Dedication and Recognition

This book is dedicated to the memory of Professor Gary Munneke, formerly of Pace University Law School. Gary was a pioneer in advancing the cause of practice management in law firms. He was also a fine teacher and mentor. A tireless advocate for those who embraced the art and science of managing law firms, Gary devoted his life to bringing out the best in everyone in his very large inner circle. He will be missed, but not forgotten.

This book is also dedicated to Fran Musselman, Dick Reed, Herb Goodfriend, and Hal Feder, in thanks for their unfailing support in my early career. I also offer special thanks to all of the many managing partners of law firms across the country who so generously gave of their time to meet with me as I gathered case material for this book. Thanks go as well to all of my clients who, over the years, gave me the opportunity to study the complexities of retirement and succession planning. I am basically a managerial economist by training, so my initial view of retirement and succession planning came from the view of "the dismal science"—with a little too much Malthusian influence. My clients helped me appreciate the emotional nature of "end-of-career" concerns, both from the point of view of the soon-to-be retiree and from the point of view of the succeeding generation of partners.

In this book, a reader might sense a bit of sympathy with the founders of law firms—and so it should be. Without them, our great legal institutions would not exist today. In many cases, the careers of founding partners are quite different from the careers of those who succeed them. They were the entrepreneurs whose vision, commitment, and willingness to invest human and cash capital enabled these great firms to emerge as established institutions. They deserve both recognition and special thanks for what they have done and continue to do to keep the profession innovative, adaptable, and diverse.

Finally, I would like to thank those persons, unknown to me, who conducted the peer review of this book. Their suggestions were very thoughtful, thorough, and helpful. Without their input, this book would be a lesser resource.

PETER A. GIULIANI
Passing the Torch
without Getting Burned
A GUIDE TO LAW FIRM RETIREMENT AND SUCCESSION PLANNING
ABA LAW PRACTICE MANAGEMENT SECTION
MARKETING • MANAGEMENT • TECHNOLOGY • FINANCE

Cover design by RIPE Creative, Inc.

Printed in the United States of America.

17 16 15 14 13   5 4 3 2 1

Library of Congress Cataloging-in-Publication Data

Giuliani, Peter A.
Passing the torch without getting burned : a guide to law firm retirement and succession planning / Peter A. Giuliani.
pages cm
Includes bibliographical references and index.
ISBN 978-1-61438-902-6
1. Lawyers--Retirement--United States. 2. Retirement--United States--Planning. 3. Practice of law--Economic aspects--United States. 4. Inheritance and succession--United States. 5. Estate planning--United States. I. Title.
KF315.G58 2013
340.068'3--dc23

2013016388

Discounts are available for books ordered in bulk. Special consideration is given to state bars, CLE programs, and other bar-related organizations. Inquire at Book Publishing, American Bar Association, 321 North Clark Street, Chicago, Illinois 60654-7598.

www.ShopABA.org

Contents

About the Author

Peter Giuliani is a partner at Smock Law Firm Consultants. His law firm management experience spans nearly forty-five years, both as a management consultant to law firms and other professional service firms, and as executive director of Cummings & Lockwood, a 180-lawyer law firm based in Stamford, Connecticut (seven years). His functional specialties include strategic planning; financial management and law firm economics; administrative and technology infrastructure planning; strategic mergers, acquisitions, and divestitures; and practice group management.

He has directed, conducted, or participated in more than 400 consulting assignments for law firms or corporate law departments involving such matters as:

- development and implementation of strategic plans;
- analysis of and consultation on strategic mergers, acquisitions, and divestitures;
- review and restructuring of partner compensation and performance evaluation;
- design and implementation of law firm organization, management, and practice group structures;
- analysis and redesign of partnership retirement and buyout plans, including valuation of partners' interests; and
- design and implementation of multitiered partnership structures.

Peter has also served as expert witness in over twenty litigation matters involving valuation of partnership interests, determination of "reasonable compensation," measurement of lost profits, and other matters.

He is the principal author of two extensive monographs on financial management of law firms, which were published by the American Bar Association in 1979, and is the recent author of "Model Partnership Agreement for New York Law Firms" (NY State Bar Association 2008). In addition, he has published dozens of articles on legal management topics, and is a regular contributor to the *Connecticut Law Tribune*.

A frequent public speaker, Peter has given more than 100 presentations to professional service groups. He has also been a regular lecturer at the New York State Bar Association's annual program, "Starting Your Own Law Practice in New York."

Prior to joining Cummings & Lockwood, Peter was a consultant with four major consulting firms. He spent five years as vice president and CFO of Altman Weil and five years as a partner in Pensa International, a firm that he helped found and that merged with Altman Weil in 1991. He was a principal and partner at Arthur Young, where he also served as National Director of Legal Consulting Services. He began his consulting career in 1968 at the New York office of Price Waterhouse, eventually focusing on law firm management issues and litigation support.

Peter has his undergraduate degree in economics from the College of the Holy Cross and an MBA in managerial economics and finance from Cornell University. He is also a Certified Public Accountant (inactive status) and a Certified Management Consultant (inactive status). In 1998, Peter was elected a Fellow of the College of Law Practice Management in recognition of his career-long dedication and contributions to improving the management of law firms. He was an active Fellow until 2012.

Introduction

• Financial and control measures in the event of death, disability or retirement.

The best time for most law firms to deal with retirement issues is very early in the life and growth of the firm. The best way to do that is to anticipate retirement and end-of-career issues as part of the process whereby the firm drafts its operating agreement.

Let's be clear. This book is not a "how-to" book or "do-it-yourself" manual for structuring a law firm retirement and succession plan. Its purpose is to identify the many variables and issues that must be considered, in the hopes that readers will better understand the scope and breadth of succession planning and dealing with end-of-career issues. While it addresses and illustrates issues regarding the valuation of a law practice, those who would take the examples and case studies in this book and try to adapt them to their own circumstances are like the guy in the well-known television commercial who is contemplating performing open-heart surgery on himself without anesthesia. The best advice is to hire a qualified expert for that task.

This book is also intended to be a companion volume to *Model Partnership Agreements for New York Law Firms*, published by the New York State Bar Association's Law Practice Management Committee (Giuliani 2008). In that book, I provided a general outline of provisions that a well-drafted law firm operating agreement should contain regarding retirement of partners. However, the subject of retirement planning is much too complex to treat in a few paragraphs of a guide on writing a partnership agreement, hence the decision to publish this book.

Throughout the course of this book, I will examine how law firms can and do create value for their owners, and suggest rational ways in which owners can be compensated for value left to the firm when they retire. I will rely both on hypothetical case studies and on "real-life" practices of existing law firms. Where possible, I will also suggest appropriate language to include in a partnership or operating agreement to govern terms of retirement and succession.

It is my hope that readers of this book will find in it a useful framework for deciding on how to deal with partner retirement and succession planning in both an economic and human-relations sense.

At the outset, however, I cannot advise strongly enough that law firms adopt a holistic approach to retirement and succession planning. At some point in every lawyer's career, she or he needs to come to terms with the fact that legal careers are finite. This is as true of sole practitioners as it is of lawyers who have hundreds of partners. Firms also need to come to terms with this fact, and encourage a free and candid discussion about individual plans. This is not to say that hard deadlines must be imposed—although many firms still have mandatory retirement or "step-down" provisions in their operating agreements—but rather that expectations need to be openly discussed as a matter of fiduciary responsibility among partners.

The orderly succession of a law practice involves a lot of candid conversation among partners (read "owners") of the business about their personal plans and expectations. It also involves careful financial and actuarial planning on the part of the continuing firm. Individual partners should seek personal financial, retirement, and estate planning advice (including advice on long-term care) from competent and experienced professionals. Finally, neither the firm nor the individual partner can ignore the most important party in the succession equation—*the client*.

When a partner retires, his or her foremost concern should be: "If I stop working, slow down, become disabled, or die, who will make sure that my clients are served?" This is especially the case with sole practitioners and partners in small firms. A competent lawyer would never advise a client to "go naked" with respect to an estate plan, so why would a competent lawyer not have a plan for protecting his or her clients at the end of his or her career? It is first and foremost a matter of ethics, not economics.

That said, this book is intended to identify key economic issues typically encountered by law firms when they consider how partners will end their careers, as they inevitably must. It also touches briefly upon the economic considerations regarding transitioning new partners into law firms. By design, this book does not address the important issues of client succession, ethical considerations, responsibilities of solo practitioners, etc. Neither does it address legal issues that might be associated with disputes over the rights of individual partners vis-à-vis their firms. The economic issues are tough enough and deserve to be considered on their own.

Chapter 1

WHY PLAN FOR RETIREMENT AND SUCCESSION?

To that familiar list of inevitable events that includes "death" and "taxes," we need to add another term—"succession." No law firm that has survived the retirement of its first generation of leadership has been able to avoid this challenging issue. Founding partners do retire, and the challenge is to ensure that their client relationships do not retire with them or simply drift away to other firms. The same is true at long-established, multigenerational firms. Rainmakers eventually retire, and the firms need to find a way to preserve client relationships.

Very often, we encounter the succession issue couched in the phraseology of a buyout plan for a senior partner. This, however, is only a small aspect of the issue—only half of the equation. Why, for example, would a law firm ever agree to pay a buyout (other than a return of capital) to someone who is leaving nothing behind? The firm might do something modest in the way of past-service recognition, or possibly as a severance arrangement to encourage someone to retire, but the basic economic proposition is that the buyout consists largely of remuneration for expected value, to be received after the person has transitioned or scaled back his or her practice.

How does one create value after transitioning from active practice? In certain types of practice, it is relatively simple. Consider the trusts and estates practitioner who leaves behind a large will vault and several trustee appointments. One hopes that, with careful client counseling and efforts on the part of the retiring partner to transition his client relationships and trustee appointments to younger lawyers, the clients' loyalties will be transferred from the individual lawyer to the firm, or at least to younger lawyers in the firm.

It is a tougher proposition, however, when we are dealing with business clients. In many instances, the relationship between the business entity and the law firm is a relationship between one of the lawyers in the firm and a leader in the business entity. If both parties are contemporaries and are both considering retirement, the problem is compounded. If the business entity is a closely-held or family business, the law firm may have already assisted the entity with succession planning. The trick is to bond the new generation of entity leaders to the new generation of lawyers.

What about a pure litigation practice? Cases come and go. They go to trial or settle. Thus, they are finite and transactional in nature. How does one leave behind something valuable that's worth paying for? The fact is, most firms that concentrate on litigation get the majority of their work through referrals from lawyers in other firms. Thus, the item of value is the referral network of the retiring lawyer. Making sure the firm gets value from the network may require the retiring lawyer to remain "of counsel" to the firm for a period of time, not really practicing law, but available to take calls from referrals. Here again, if the lawyer's referral network consists of his or her contemporaries, the network may also be retiring.

In planning for succession, one needs to understand these basic economic considerations. Whether a law firm has a mandatory retirement plan or an informal "understanding" about when lawyers should begin thinking about bonding their clients to the firm, there are several issues to think about. Here's a partial list:

1. At what point in a partner's career is it appropriate for the firm to introduce the matter of succession planning, presuming that some partners might choose to "self-initiate" the discussion?
2. How does the firm fairly compensate—both prior to and after transition—those partners who plan for transitioning clients and successfully execute their plans?
3. How does the firm fairly compensate those partners who inherit client relationships from transitioning partners, and how does it make sure the inheriting partner is the right person for the relationship?
4. Should there be different protocols that govern "self-initiated" succession plans and "firm-initiated" plans?

5. What are the details of the post-transition relationship between the former partner and the firm (e.g., office and secretarial support, compensation for work done on behalf of the firm or its clients, how the former partner is presented to clients and the general public, continuing rights and responsibilities of former partners, etc.)?
6. What is the protocol for handling special cases, such as a partner who voluntarily steps out of equity status, but assumes a continuing, albeit reduced, role with the firm?

These are largely economic and procedural topics. Dealing with retiring partners, especially firm founders, is usually an emotional proposition, especially if the succession discussion is "firm-initiated." However, such discussions are inevitable. Handled sensitively and well, the arrangements can benefit both the firm and the retiree. There needs to be an atmosphere of mutual trust and candor on both sides of the table.

In any law firm's history, there are at least four critical events:

1. The founding of the firm;
2. The admission of the first nonfounding partner(s);
3. The death, disability, retirement, or withdrawal of one or more founding partners;
4. The death, disability, retirement, or withdrawal of one or more nonfounding partners.

Death and disability are easier to deal with economically, as they are insurable events. The economics of retirement, on the other hand, are complicated by two important considerations:

1. Who is retiring (i.e., founder or nonfounder)?
2. What value is the retiring partner leaving to the firm?

This is not a book about the legal and contractual aspects of how law firms reach agreements with their partners about retirement. It is really a book about the economics of retirement planning. It is important to understand that founders of law firms make a different economic contribution to their law firms than do the partners who follow them in later years. However, for founders to reap some of the economic value they created by setting up a law firm, they must leave behind a viable, healthy, and well-managed entity that can carry on the firm's business. Only then can the succeeding partners afford to fund the transition to the next generation.

This is not to say that succeeding partners do not create economic value. They do. Yet, mostly they do so by standing on the shoulders of those who took the financial risk of forming the firm in the first place. They may bring lateral practices with them that add new value to the firm, but normally that value is recognized by the compensation the firm has paid to attract them. Homegrown partners may create value by adding new skills, but the investment in building those skills has been financed by the founders. They would not have built the skills for the firm, had the founders not created the firm to support them.

If law firms want to provide a retirement benefit for nonfounders, they can do so either through a qualified retirement plan, a funded or unfunded nonqualified plan, or a combination of both. I strongly advise law firms to take full advantage of tax-deferred qualified retirement plans before considering other types of retirement plans. As future chapters will point out, economically successful retirement plans all depend upon the ages of the partners when the plans are adopted. Younger partners have a long "runway" ahead of them and can more easily plan personally for retirement. Older partners have shorter "runways." Law partnerships need to keep these conditions in mind when considering alternatives.

Law firms are excellent vehicles for building reasonably good annual incomes. They are singularly lousy vehicles for creating wealth for their owners. Unless and until a market exists in which investors can trade in the shares of law firms, there will be no way to "cash out." Law firms are also fragile businesses because the clients and lawyers who sustain them can walk out the door at any time, so in most cases "buyers" of law firms—i.e., continuing partners, lateral partners, acquiring law firms, et al.—are probably not interested in paying large cash premiums for "goodwill" or "going-concern" value. Quite simply, there is no pot of gold at the end of the rainbow, as there might be with another type of commercial enterprise.

Perhaps the simplest economic strategy is "Naked In/Naked Out." Using this strategy, the law firm sets up a qualified defined-contribution or cash-balance retirement plan, optimizes the current incomes of the partners so they can contribute the maximum to their plans, and returns their accumulated capital at retirement. This is clean and simple from an economic point of view, but unfortunately it ignores the "soft values" created by partners who leave behind referral networks, proprietary intellectual property, and loyal "institutionalized" client relationships.

Successful retirement and succession planning involves managing a whole integrated array of moving parts to achieve an end result that is humane, fair, affordable, and ethical. Humane, in the sense that it takes into account the emotions of the retiring partner. Fair, in the sense that it balances the interests of the retiree and the continuing partners. Affordable, in the sense that it does not place an undue burden on the continuing firm. Ethical, in the sense that it puts the interests of clients and the continuing firm's ability to serve them above all other considerations.

For many career professionals, retirement can be a very emotional step. In ancient Rome, when a triumphant general paraded through the streets among cheering throngs, a slave was said to follow him closely from behind and murmur, "Memento mori," which means "Remember you will die." Thus, hubris was tempered by interjecting a humbling thought.

As we professionals approach the ends of our careers, we all have our "memento mori" moments, and facing retirement may be one of them. Deep down, the partner may regret that his skills and energy are not what they once were. He may also feel underappreciated by a new generation of younger partners, many of whom he trained and mentored. Clients and close personal friends may have retired or passed on, leaving the partner feeling gradually more isolated. These feelings, together with a host of other anxieties, can combine to make the thought of retiring from practice and leaving behind one's longtime and familiar business environment a prospect fraught with emotional conflict.

This is why retirement and succession planning need to be handled humanely by the continuing partners. They need to recognize that they will eventually be in the same position as the retiring partner. One hopes that they will treat the retiring partner in the same manner in which they would like to be treated when it is their turn to face the inescapable end-of-career circumstance.

The issue of fairness is a matter of perception. I have seen instances in which a founder expects a substantial buyout when he or she retires, but has always insisted that he or she be the highest-paid partner, year after year. Now, if the continuing partners' perception is that the retiring partner has misused his or her position to command premium pay over the years, but has really not deserved that pay, they will be reluctant to agree to a substantial "buyout." In their minds, the perceived unfair pay level has already compensated the outgoing partner for his or her "buyout."

Contrast that situation with one in which the outgoing partner's compensation has been gradually scaling down (voluntarily or by reason of firm compensation policy decisions) in the years leading up to retirement. Continuing partners may, in such a circumstance, feel more favorably disposed toward paying some kind of buyout or retirement benefit.

Thus, the notion of "fairness" is colored by the perceptions as to how the partner has behaved over his or her career. If a partner has always exhibited "firm-first" behavior, mentored and trained younger lawyers, shared clients with others, contributed positively and selflessly to firm management, and otherwise comported himself or herself as a co-owner of the business, the next generation is more likely to look favorably on him or her than they would have had he or she consistently behaved selfishly or egotistically.

Simply stated, a retirement or buyout plan should be considered "affordable" if it does not significantly impair the ongoing firm's ability to pay competitive compensation to its continuing partners. Stated alternatively, one must ask the question, "What is a reasonable amount of money for a law firm to spend on paying retirement benefits to its former partners?"

For most law firms, affordability is not a big issue if one partner retires every four or five years. It becomes a major issue, however, if the firm is facing multiple retirements in a relatively short period of time. This is the problem confronting many large firms that adopted unfunded defined-benefit retirement plans in the 1950s (see Chapter 2). Today, consultants see an increasing number of law firms struggling to deal with "bunching" of retirements as the baby boomers start to retire and as partners who have already retired live much longer than they have in the past. (For a lighthearted article on how we got a "normal retirement age" of sixty-five, see Mary-Lou Weisman's *New York Times* article, "The History of Retirement, From Early Man to A.A.R.P.")

What, then, is considered "normal" for payments to retired partners? Most unfunded pension plans cap annual payments to former partners at between 3 percent and 4 percent of the firm's annual net income. Any amounts owed in excess of the cap usually carry forward to future years, although there are a few exceptions to that rule, as well.

Another benchmark of affordability might be the actual spending of law firms on payments to former partners. An analysis of several years of large firm data from the annual economic surveys conducted by PricewaterhouseCoopers (the survey is published only to participants and is not publicly available) reveals that the average large law firm (250 lawyers and up) spends about 1.2 perecent of its gross revenue annually on payments to retired partners. The average survey firm reported a ratio of net income to revenue of 40 percent, so that would convert the 1.2 percent of revenue to 3.0 percent of net income (i.e., 1.2 percent divided by 40 percent). Note that this is in line with the caps included in unfunded plans.

It should go without saying that any retirement plan that is considered humane, fair, and affordable must also be ethical, in the sense that it should not interfere with the retiree's or the firm's duties to put client interests first. Thus, even though it may be possible for one law firm to acquire another law firm (see Rule 1.17 of the ABA *Model Rules of Professional Conduct*), it may not "acquire" the other firm's clients, since the client always has the right to select counsel.

Some retirement plans do, however, pay modest bonus compensation to retired partners based upon how much revenue is generated, post-retirement, from clients that they had "originated" while they were actively practicing. This would appear to be permitted by the Model Rules, as the client still has the right to select counsel.

That said, while the retirement plan may be strictly ethical under the Model Rules, firms and retirees should make sure that payments to retired partners do not create some kind of perverse incentive that might create the *appearance* of unethical behavior. For example, if the succession plan involves selling an estates and trusts practice to another firm, the plan should probably not provide direct financial incentives that reward the retiring partner for "steering" fiduciary appointments to the successor firm. Presumably, the value of potential fiduciary appointments has already been factored into the valuation of the practice at the time of acquisition.

In summary, succession and retirement planning are necessary activities for all law practices of all sizes. Such planning needs to consider emotional and ethical factors, as well as economic factors. While we may comment from time to time on emotional and ethical concerns in these pages, this book is mostly about economic concerns.

Chapter 2

A BRIEF HISTORY OF PARTNER RETIREMENT PLANS

Until World War II, law firms made no retirement or pension provisions for their partners. In those days, most law firms compensated partners either with equal shares of profits or according to a strict seniority-based lockstep compensation system. All partners were required to contribute capital—often substantial sums—to finance the firm's operations. Law firms never borrowed money. All partners were jointly and severally liable for any and all acts of malpractice and for commercial obligations, such as office leases. Consequently, the door to partnership opened only infrequently and only to those thought to be the most thoughtful and careful practitioners. Partnership was viewed as a lifetime tenure and partners generally never switched firms.

Because law partners were both jointly and severally liable for commercial obligations and professional malpractice, there was a feeling that firms had to operate from a single office and that partnerships could not grow too large, lest the partners collectively lose sight of one another's doings. The then presiding partner of Cravath, Swaine & Moore, Mr. Royall Victor, Jr., in 1969 explained to me that a law firm could not exist with more than 100 lawyers. He reasoned that a partnership with more than twenty-five partners would not be able to function properly—a quality control and communication issue—and that, since one needed three associates for every partner, the firm could be no larger than one hundred lawyers.

When a partner retired (virtually no partners withdrew from their firms to practice law elsewhere), he (there were no female partners) received his share of income earned prior to the date of retirement, plus whatever balance had accumulated in his capital account. Many partners worked well into their seventies or eighties and, with male life expectancies being what they were, most died before they chose to retire.

During the 1950s and 1960s, General Motors and other major corporations began providing their workers with pension benefits similar to those offered by the railroads, and law firms began to consider how they might provide some benefit to retiring partners. Many firms combined a partner retirement plan with a policy of mandatory retirement, coupled with a "scale-down" period during which the partner was expected to gradually reduce his work schedule, transfer clients to others, and eventually "wind up" his practice. Typically, the mandatory retirement age was set at seventy, with "scale-down" starting at age sixty-five. Under certain circumstances, partners could elect to retire early, with reduced benefits.

For most larger firms (a "large" firm was typically about twenty-five or thirty lawyers), partner compensation was strictly a matter of seniority. New partners started at the bottom of the "ladder" and gradually moved up a "rung" each year for about eight years until they reached parity with the more senior partners. The highest-paid partner typically made about four times what the newest partner made. When it came time to "scale down," a partner's sharing percentage was reduced by 20 percent each year over a five-year period, until the partner retired. Once he retired, he then received an annual pension for life. If he predeceased his wife, she would continue to receive his pension benefit for ten additional years or until she died.

The amount of the pension benefit was typically 25 percent of the average of the partner's highest five years of compensation prior to entering "scale-down." For example, a partner who earned an average of $200,000 during his highest five compensation years would receive a lifetime pension of $50,000 per year. To protect the firm, aggregate payments to all retired partners in any one year were typically capped at 4 percent of distributable net income. Any obligations that could not be paid in one year were rolled forward to the next.

Such unfunded pension arrangements were, for the most part, considered to be affordable and never even came close to hitting the 4 percent cap. Consider, for example, that firms elevated associates to partnership far less frequently than they do today, and that firms adhered to a strict "up-or-out" policy when it came to those who didn't make the grade. Most firms also had effective "alumni" programs in which passed-over associates were placed in in-house positions at firm clients, where possible.

Typically, a new partner might be admitted every two or three years. Multiple admissions in a single year were rare. In addition, life expectancies were much shorter. It was rare that a partner would live much more than five years after retiring, and his widow would probably outlive him by no more than a few years. Consequently, the likelihood that the firm would be paying out multiple pensions year after year was quite small, and most retirees and surviving spouses never collected much more than six or seven years of benefits.

In smaller firms, especially those in which the founding partners were still practicing, the retirement benefit was calculated as a purchase of the partner's interest in the firm. In addition to receiving his share of undistributed income and the balance of his capital account, a retiring partner would "sell" his interest in unbilled work and accounts receivable to the firm. Some firms actually tried to keep track of each partner's ownership interest in unbilled and uncollected accounts in a "memorandum account" by measuring the increase or decrease in these two assets each year, multiplying each partner's sharing percentage by the difference, and either crediting or debiting the resulting amount to each partner's "memorandum account." (Such plans were typically designed for and used by accounting firms, including many of the then "Big Eight" firms.) When he retired, a partner would be paid the value of his "memorandum account" in sixty equal monthly installments.

A simpler approach adopted by some firms was to use a multiple of earnings to compute the value of a partner's interest. A typical plan would be to pay an amount equal to three times the average of the partner's highest five years of compensation in 120 equal monthly installments. Thus, a partner earning an average of $200,000 per year would receive a retirement benefit of $60,000 per year for ten years.

Both of these plans were to be funded from future earnings and both typically had limits on how much could be paid out in a single year. Again, with partnerships being relatively small and restricted, these plans rarely, if ever, posed a problem.

In the 1970s and early 1980s, it became possible for small corporations to set up qualified defined-benefit pension plans that, for all practical purposes, covered only the shareholders of the corporation. In fact, it was possible to adopt such a plan for a corporation with only one shareholder. Such plans were very attractive because they allowed shareholders to put away large tax-deductible contributions that would continue to grow on a tax-deferred basis until retirement.

During this period, smaller law firms and individual partners in large firms began to incorporate in order to take advantage of these retirement plans. They were also attracted to the limited liability protection offered by incorporating. Ultimately, the government caught up with these discriminatory plans and passed the ERISA regulations that require such plans to cover all employees, thus rendering these types of plans unaffordable.

Throughout the '70s and '80s, lots of other things were happening to U.S. law firms that would overturn the old paradigms and lay the foundation for how law firms are structured today. Among the more important developments were:

- the rapid growth of law firms everywhere;
- proliferation of branch offices, with large firms in cities like Cleveland, Philadelphia, and San Francisco leading the charge;
- increased partner and practice group mobility among firms;
- the disappearance of general partnerships in favor of corporations (initially) and limited liability partnerships (eventually), as the favored entity choice for law firms;
- the emergence of multitiered partnerships to accommodate alternative career paths and hang on to "specialty talent," among other reasons (For a more extensive discussion of multitier partnerships, see Appendix A.);
- consolidation of firms through mergers and acquisitions;
- a major shift away from egalitarian reward systems to more merit-based systems;
- the gradual aging of the baby boom generation partners; and
- increased reliance on defined-contribution retirement savings plans (SEPs, IRAs, 401(k)s, etc.) accompanied by a decline in the use of unfunded and qualified defined-benefit pension plans.

The 1990s and the 2000s witnessed even greater shifts in the legal profession. To start with, there have been three recessions in the last quarter century. The first was triggered by the collapse of the savings and loan industry shortly after the stock market nosedive on October 19, 1987. The second was directly tied to the bursting of the dot-com and technology bubbles shortly after the Y2K nonevent. Then came the "Great Recession" that followed the bursting of the housing bubble and the ensuing financial services sector collapse.

Up until the recession of 1987, law firms had been largely considered recession-proof. When business was up, transactional practices thrived. When the business cycle turned down, litigation and bankruptcy picked up the slack. These countercyclical practices made for relatively stable businesses, because lawyers would shift from deal work to litigation and work-outs, then in the ensuing recovery switch back.

Unlike prior recessions, however, the last three have profoundly affected law firms. In all three, firms first reacted by cutting support staff. Then, they fired associates, sometimes laying off entire classes of new hires. During the first two recoveries, there were frenzied rounds of associate lateral hiring, as firms struggled to fill experience gaps that resulted from the layoffs. Twice in this period, these hiring frenzies also triggered spikes in associate starting salaries. So, when the Great Recession hit, firms in major money centers found themselves once again bloated with high-priced new hires whose cost they could not pass on to clients. There was some ripple effect across other markets, but the legal market recession was initially probably more of a Wall Street phenomenon than a Main Street one.

Another significant change happened during the Great Recession. Firms everywhere started questioning whether partnership status meant lifetime tenure. The last several years have seen a slowdown in the rate of law-school hiring at bigger firms, a flattening of the growth in associate salaries, a modest bump in lateral associate hiring, and a huge increase in lateral mobility among equity partners with large books of portable business.

Simultaneously, there has been a rising trend toward "de-equitization" as well as the outplacement of midlevel and older partners whose practices have not recovered from losses sustained during the recession.

The net result is that law firms are facing new economic realities. Clients are putting pressure on fees. Partners are even more willing to move to higher-paying firms. Associates are questioning whether the personal sacrifices required to rise to equity partnership are really worth it. In short, in 2013 we are witnessing a gradual shift in the basic business model that served law firms so well from the 1950s through the 1980s.

How, then, are retirement and succession plans affected by these events, based upon market observations? First, on the succession front, some firms have begun offering unfunded early retirement packages to partners whose practices are not recovering from the recession. Other firms are simply firing partners for the first time in their histories.

Second, those firms that still have unfunded, nonqualified retirement plans (holdovers from the 1950s) are realizing that the plans are becoming unaffordable. Younger partners realize that they will be working many years to finance the retirements of more senior partners. They are being wooed away by competing firms that do not have such retirement plans. Furthermore, these types of plans have become "poison pills" in law firm merger discussions. For example, a law firm that does not have an unfunded plan—or has just terminated such a plan—is going to be very reluctant to merge with another firm that still has such a plan in place.

Third, even funded, qualified plans are in growing trouble. When some firms terminated their unfunded plans, they replaced them with qualified defined-benefit plans. These plans were hit with a "double whammy" because of falling interest rates and investment returns. The investment portfolios that hold the assets to fund these plans lost a lot of value over the years and have not risen back to the values their trustees had anticipated. At the same time, record low interest rates have reduced the discount rates that pension funds are required to use to compute the present value of accrued plan benefits (essentially the plan liability). Lower discount rates result in higher liability values. Lower investment returns result in lower asset values. The result is that many of these qualified plans are woefully underfunded.

This creates a perverse incentive for partners to jump ship to other firms that do not offer qualified defined-benefit plans. In the case of nonqualified, defined-benefit plans, defecting partners generally forfeit their retirement benefits when they move to other firms. In qualified plans, by contrast, benefits are portable once the partner has satisfied vesting requirements. So, for example, a partner can leave Firm A to join Firm B without giving up his or her retirement benefit and, in so defecting, leave the job of funding his or her vested benefits—or making up for an underfunded plan—to Firm A's partners.

In summary, partnership has ceased to be a lifetime commitment on the part of both partners and their law firms. No longer is it expected that lawyers will practice at the same firm for their entire careers. Also, partners who are not "measuring up" can face de-equitization and even dismissal by their firms. More important, the notion of joint and several liability has been abandoned to facilitate more rapid growth by lateral acquisition.

All this means that law firms are far less paternalistic than they were in the early days. The "cultural glue" that once held firms together has eroded as the markets for legal services and high-quality legal talent have become more competitive.

The robust appetite for growth among law firms since the 1960s drew heavily on the baby boom generation. As these lawyers became partners in large numbers, they created a real actuarial problem for the traditional unfunded pension plans adopted by many law firms. Many more partners would be retiring at the same time, and most of them would be expected to live much longer than the generation that preceded them. Eventually, the demographics of most law partnerships would overwhelm their retirement plans.

As firms continued to accelerate growth at an even faster pace by merging or being acquired, the unfunded or underfunded liabilities inherent in traditional retirement plans became the "poison pill" that killed many a deal. Eventually, they will have to go, and unwinding them will be a painful and difficult task.

That said, there are still many firms around that have unfunded plans, and the liabilities are growing. In fact, any law firm that was founded before World War II probably has or had such a plan in place. One need only read the business and legal press articles about the woes of New York's Dewey & LeBoeuf LLP to understand what happens when a law firm tries to finance aggressive lateral growth, partner compensation guarantees, and a growing unfunded pension liability out of the same profit stream, combined with a highly leveraged balance sheet. Eventually, something has to give.

These concerns, of course, have been more of an issue for larger firms. Meanwhile, smaller firms have become more prevalent. Tired of "big-firm blues," many associates and younger partners left the security of larger firms to open smaller, more entrepreneurial firms. Other firms were founded in less-populous communities that could support only a few relatively small firms. Today, many of these entrepreneurial firms have become quite successful, and in many cases, their founding partners have achieved greater economic success than they would have achieved at their former firms.

Martindale-Hubbell currently lists about 83,000 law firms in the United States. Of those firms, 92 percent consist of firms with fewer than twenty-five lawyers and 80 percent have fewer than ten lawyers. This has always been the general profile of the legal profession. That said, it is my experience that the number of larger firms is shrinking because of increased merger and acquisition activity and consolidation at that end of the market. From my perspective, the rate of formation of smaller firms is on the rise. The reasons behind these trends are beyond the scope of this book, but the trends are, nevertheless, worth noting.

Unfortunately, many entrepreneurial lawyers are so highly focused on getting their new firms off the ground that they sometimes lose sight of the need to plan an exit or succession strategy for themselves. Consequently, many partnership and shareholder agreements that are drafted when these firms are set up are either silent on the question of retirement/succession, or have provisions that fail to anticipate the changing views of the original partners as they approach the end of their working careers.

Trying to develop and implement succession plans when the most senior partners are already approaching the ends of their careers can be quite problematic, especially if the younger partners are caught off guard by older partners' requests for buyouts or retirement compensation. The best time for most law firms to deal with these issues is very early in the life and growth of a firm.

Throughout this book, live examples will show that creative retirement plans can and do work, but only if there is enough time to build up retirement reserves or other assets to fund the plans. In this day and age, however, the notion that a firm can adopt a plan whereby retirements are funded out of future earnings is untenable. There are simply too many factors that contribute to the inability of most firms—especially smaller ones—to meet post-retirement obligations.

Perhaps the biggest factor is partner mobility. All too often, we hear of a law firm collapsing because its biggest producers decided to leave, rather than shoulder the burden of financing retirement benefits owed to retiring partners. In the old days, when all partners were held jointly and severally liable for their firm's professional and commercial liabilities, contractual pension obligations—a commercial liability of the firm—could follow defecting partners to other firms. Now that firms practice under limited liability entities, it is doubtful that remaining partners could hold defectors liable. The only protection is probably a clause in the operating agreement that allows nondefectors to force a dissolution of the firm rather than allow defectors to jump ship and leave liabilities behind.

All the more reason to be sure that firms have plans in place that will fund buyouts or retiree pensions and that those plans are put in place as early as possible in the life of a firm. This ensures that the "rules of play" are known in advance and that partners generally self-fund most of their own retirement benefits while they are still in active practice.

Chapter 3

SURVEY OF AGREEMENT TERMS

At this point, it might be helpful to provide a summary of all the significant economic issues that should go into a retirement/succession plan and consider how a lot of other firms—mostly smaller ones—have dealt with them. As part of the effort that went into writing this book, I interviewed and/or surveyed over seventy-five law firms from all over the country—mostly under 100 lawyers—to compare how they dealt with retirement and buyout issues. These firms covered a wide range of practice types, from general practices to boutiques and from plaintiff oriented to defense oriented. While this research can hardly claim to be comprehensive, it can provide a useful overview of how different firms address the same set of issues.

In reviewing the survey/interview data, it became fairly clear that most firms' provisions, if they have provisions, fit within two basic types of plans: a buyout of a partner's interest or a retirement benefit plan that substitutes for a purchase of the partner's ownership interest in firm net assets. Note that, by nature, most of these plans are not prefunded, per se, but rely on the eventual collection of unbilled and uncollected accounts. They are subject to problems with "bunching" when a number of partners are scheduled to retire at the same time, so many of these plans cap payments to retired partners at 3 percent to 4 percent of each year's net income. Any missed payments roll over into future years.

The table that follows summarizes the different provisions most typically found under each alternative plan.

Table 1.1 Comparative Analysis of Selected Partnership Agreement Provisions

Partnership Agreement Issue/Provision	Alternative A: Buyout	Alternative B: Retirement Benefit
Valuation of Firm Cash Capital	Cash-basis book value per firm's general ledger and/or tax return.	Cash-basis book value per firm's general ledger and/or tax return.
Percentages of Capital Interest	Always kept in proportion to current profit participation percentages. Accounts adjusted annually to prevent dilution of interests of existing partners by creation of new units.	May be kept in proportion to profit percentages, but there is no requirement that accumulated capital and current earnings be proportional.
Voting Provisions	Firms are about evenly split between weighted voting and one vote per partner.	No requirement that voting follow income or capital shares. Voting provisions are generally driven by governance considerations rather than any sense of "equity."
Basis for Valuation of Termination/ Retirement Interest	Current undistributed earnings, plus cash capital and accumulated interest thereon, plus share of unbilled work in progress and accounts receivable at estimated realizable value as of separation date.	Current undistributed earnings plus capital account and accumulated interest. Retirement benefit is considered to be in lieu of buyout of partnership interest. Most firms base retirement benefit on an average of the partners' highest three to five earning years, adjusted for inflation.
Basis for Valuing Partners' Required Capital	Initial capital assessment and subsequent "calls" are based upon the firm's need for working capital. Partners are assessed pro rata based upon current income percentages. No attempt is made to keep ownership percentages in line with current income percentages.	Initial capital assessment and subsequent "calls" are based upon the firm's need for working capital. Partners are assessed pro rata based upon current income percentages. No attempt is made to keep ownership percentages in line with current income percentages.

Partnership Agreement Issue/Provision	Alternative A: Buyout	Alternative B: Retirement Benefit
Retirement Provisions	Taxable and nontaxable portions of buyout are computed separately and paid out monthly over thirty-six to sixty months. Priority is given to return of capital. Buyout is payable to the partner or his or her estate, should he or she die before receiving the full amount. Voluntary retirement ages range from sixty to sixty-five years. Mandatory ages range from sixty-five to seventy years. About 60 percent of firms have mandatory retirement provisions. Partners over retirement age may petition the firm to be permitted to stay on in some capacity. About 50 percent of firms provide for paid "of counsel" status for retired partners. A few firms have adopted provisions for early retirement at age fifty-five, both voluntary and forced. Benefit is often discounted in cases of early retirement.	Note: These provisions are in addition to any interest the partner might have in the firm's qualified plan(s). Capital is returned within six months to one year. Partner immediately begins receiving monthly retirement benefit check (fully taxable). Most common practice is to pay a "time-certain" annual benefit, based upon average terminal compensation. Voluntary retirement ages range from sixty to sixty-five years. Mandatory ages range from sixty-five to seventy years. About 60 percent of firms have mandatory retirement provisions. Partners over retirement age may petition the firm to be permitted to stay on in some capacity. About 50 percent of firms provide for paid "of counsel" status for retired partners. A few firms have adopted provisions for early retirement at age fifty-five, both voluntary and forced. Benefit is often discounted in cases of early retirement.
Provisions for Death Prior to Retirement	Payments to the estate as though partner had retired.	Cash capital is returned. Payment of retirement benefits to the estate for a fixed period of time.
Provisions for Permanent Disability Prior to Retirement	Payments to the partner as though he or she had retired.	Cash capital is returned. Payment of retirement benefits until death or a date certain. There is rarely a surviving spouse benefit for some period of time after death.

Partnership Agreement Issue/Provision	Alternative A: Buyout	Alternative B: Retirement Benefit
Provisions for Voluntary Withdrawal—Noncompetition	Payments to the partner as though he or she had retired.	Cash capital is returned. To the extent the partner has satisfied vesting requirements, the present value of retirement benefits is paid out or is deferred until attainment of retirement age at the option of the partner.
Provisions for Voluntary Withdrawal—Competition	Return of cash capital account and current share of undistributed income. Many firms make no distinction between competitive and noncompetitive withdrawal because they believe noncompete agreements are unenforceable.	Return of cash capital account and current share of undistributed income. Many firms make no distinction between competitive and noncompetitive withdrawal because they believe noncompete agreements are unenforceable.
Provisions for Expulsion of a Partner	Forfeiture of all benefits.	Forfeiture of all benefits.

Please remember that this table merely attempts to summarize what other firms have done. This in no way recommends these terms as best practices. Each firm will have to design its own plan, based upon its particular circumstances.

Whatever the structure of the partnership agreement provisions, it is important to consider how the eventual payments will be funded. Previously, we stated that most such provisions anticipate that the payments will be funded by the eventual collection of unbilled and uncollected accounts. A few firms—about 10 percent of this sample group—have created a mechanism to set aside some funding prior to partners retiring.

Perhaps the most common method is to purchase life insurance policies that will accumulate value over the years. When a partner retires, the firm usually applies the cash value of the policy to at least partially pay for the retirement benefit.

Only one or two firms actually set aside money each year to eventually fund retirements. To accomplish this, they withhold a small percentage of otherwise distributable earnings and carry this amount as "restricted capital" on the firm's balance sheet.

Neither of these techniques is efficient from a tax perspective, as the insurance premiums or capital withholdings are not deductible expenses.

Chapter 4

THE SPECIAL CASE OF THE FOUNDING PARTNERS

In a purely economic sense, founders present one of the most challenging succession issues. As most successful businesspeople know, starting up a commercial enterprise—and a law firm is a commercial enterprise—requires capital. First, there are expenditures required for "brick-and-mortar": the office space, furniture, library, computer and telephone equipment, copiers and other office equipment, etc. Next come expenditures needed to build an identity for the firm: letterhead, website, signage, directory listings, notices to clients and referral sources, etc. Finally, and probably most significantly, capital is required to finance operations while the firm's practice is ramping up. This challenge is probably best understood through a case study.

The Crusoe Law Firm

A CASE STUDY OF A START-UP

Rob Crusoe had been at Crumb & Crumb for eight years. A bright young associate, Rob was a rising star at the firm. But Rob always had an entrepreneurial itch, having begun his working career in the business world while he put himself through law school. He was thirty-eight years old and wanted to build his own law firm.

Over the years, Rob had developed a lot of clients, contacts, and referral sources who had great faith and trust in his abilities as a lawyer. Privately, they had assured him that they would support him, if he ever chose to start his own firm. They realized that a lot of the money they paid Crumb & Crumb for Rob's services went to cover the firm's substantial overhead. It was their belief that Rob, with the help of a good associate, could continue to provide the same quality service at lower cost.

After notifying the Crumb & Crumb partners of his intent to strike out on his own, Rob began thinking about what he would need to launch a new law firm. To start, he needed an associate. For four years, Rob had been working hard to train and develop Billie Friday, one of C&C's better young associates. Although younger and less experienced than Rob, Billie also had a dream of working at a small firm and building it into something bigger. So when Rob approached Billie with an offer, she was eager to accept.

Rob and Billie settled on a compensation package that amounted to $150,000 per year, including her medical benefits and malpractice insurance. If everything worked out well, Rob said, he would also pay Billie a $15,000 bonus at year-end.

Rob was comfortable with this arrangement, because he knew he could attract enough business to eventually produce fees in the range of $50,000 per month, once everything was up and running. He also felt comfortable about his ability to attract enough new work in twelve months to boost fees to $65,000 per month.

Rob knew that the first four months would be lean, because he and Billie had to market to referral sources and former clients before matters would begin to come in at a sufficient pace. Once they got working on matters, it would take about two months to be able to bill clients and another two months for clients to pay them.

With his associate lined up, Rob then recruited his secretary from C&C to be his assistant and office manager in the new firm. Betty had worked for both Rob and Billie. Giving Betty a raise for her expanded responsibilities brought her compensation package to $75,000 per year, including payroll taxes and benefits.

Rather than lay out a lot of money to buy office furnishings, Rob was able to negotiate a deal for a fully furnished space at the rate of $75,000 per year. He was also able to lease all the telephones, computers, and office equipment, thus further avoiding a second large capital investment. The equipment leases and other office overhead were estimated to run about $25,000 per year. For malpractice insurance, premises insurance, personal liability coverage, and other costs, Rob budgeted an additional $15,000 per year.

Next, Rob took a long, hard look at his own needs. His wife had a good job, and between her salary and some money he had inherited from his grandfather, Rob and his wife could make ends meet for several months. Her employer provided medical insurance, so that cost was also covered. Once the firm's profits reached $12,000 per month, Rob felt he could begin paying himself a draw of $10,000 per month, leaving any excess cash in the firm to fund operations through the end of the year. He also felt he needed to budget $15,000 per year for business development expenses.

Having done all his planning, Rob decided to prepare a budget for the new firm so he could judge what everything would look like once it got up and running. Here was the result of his projection:

ROB'S PROJECTION

Estimated Revenue	780,000
Estimated Costs	
Associate	(165,000)
Secretary	(75,000)
Office Rent and Occupancy	(75,000)
Other Overhead	(25,000)
Insurance, etc.	(15,000)
Business Development	(15,000)
Partner Draw	(120,000)
Estimated Profit	290,000
Partner Draw	120,000
Total Partner Compensation	410,000

Needless to say, Rob was quite pleased with this result. Even if his estimate of profit was off by a factor of 25 percent, he would consider himself successful.

Having done his homework, Rob thought it might be a good idea to share his plan with Tim Sleevegarter, his trusted accountant. It was Tim who delivered Rob his big surprise.

"Rob, this is a fine goal," said Tim, "but you've got a lot of pain to go through before you can get there. If you're right about how long it will take to develop the business and start getting paid by clients, you won't earn a dime of profit for eight months. Look at your first twelve months."

THE ACCOUNTANT'S PROJECTION

Month	Fees Collected	Operating Costs	Net Profit
1		30,833	(30,833)
2		30,833	(30,833)
3		30,833	(30,833)
4		30,833	(30,833)
5		30,833	(30,833)
6		30,833	(30,833)
7	5,000	30,833	(25,833)
8	20,000	30,833	(10,833)
9	35,000	30,833	4,167
10	45,000	30,833	14,167
11	50,000	30,833	19,167
12	50,000	30,833	19,167

"You won't be able to take a draw until October. More importantly, before you make the first dollar of profit, you'll have to carry all of the firm's operating costs. That's an investment of $222,000 before things start to turn around!"

Rob replied, "Well, things get better after that, don't they?"

"Sure they do," agreed Tim. "But your money is going to be tied up for two years before you get it back, assuming you need to pay yourself a draw. By that time, you'll probably want to add another associate, and you'll have to finance him or her the same way you financed the firm. Every time you add someone you have to carry his or her salary and support costs for somewhere between six and eight months, depending on how quickly you can get the person busy. That is a very real capital investment, but it's not readily obvious."

"Gee, Tim, will I ever get back all of my investments if I keep on growing the firm? What happens if I bring in Billie as a partner?"

"Then Billie will have to share some of the cost of financing the firm's growth in the future. That's a good thing, but she should have to invest some of her own cash to pay you back for your investment. Eventually, financing growth will get easier, but you took the big risk and put up all the capital in the first place. You should get your investment back, plus a hefty return for putting the firm together and being its banker."

At the end of the first year, Rob's firm will have accumulated $150,000 in accounts receivable, plus another $150,000 in unbilled work. Eventually, this "inventory" will be billed and collected, but it will also be replaced by more "inventory" as long as the firm's workload remains stable or continues to grow. If, for example, Rob's expectations come true and the firm starts to produce at the rate of $65,000 per month, "inventory" at the end of two years will have ballooned to $390,000.

For every percentage-point increase in monthly activity, Rob's investment in "inventory" increases $3,900. If after two years, Rob is able to negotiate a 5 percent rate increase with his clients, his investment in "inventory" will have increased another $19,500.

This story illustrates why founding partners are often treated differently from other partners who come into the firm after them. They have to finance the firm's start-up as well as all of the early-stage growth in the firm.

Experience shows, however, that partners who are admitted years after the firm was founded fail to appreciate what it took to create the firm in the first place. The lesson for founders is to make sure that when they set up the firm they provide a way to eventually get their investment back. It's a much tougher sell to younger partners if one waits forty years to bring up the subject.

In Chapter 1, I wrote about the concepts of affordability and fairness—or at least the perception of fairness. Waiting until late in one's career to introduce the subject of a "buyout," deferred compensation plan, or retirement payments inevitably raises questions of affordability and fairness. For example, if the retiring founder's practice has been in decline for several years, the succeeding partners will be rightly concerned as to whether the firm can afford much of a payout. The expected profits of the firm may be insufficient to finance the payout because the retiring founder may be leaving little by way of a legacy practice when he or she ceases working.

This situation gets even more complicated if the firm has one or two other founders who are likely to retire within a few years of the first founder. If the firm has not addressed the issues of retirement and expectations of the founders, it is likely whatever deal is struck with the first founder to retire will be expected to set a precedent for the other founders. The bunching of retirements also compounds the issue of affordability. If the continuing firm has concerns about the affordability of one founder's benefit, adding one or two other founders to the mix—each expecting the same arrangement as was created for the first founder—can trigger a crisis that might encourage younger partners to leave the firm rather than stay around to fund multiple retirements.

It is also important for founders to recognize that, if they expect to be paid a buyout or pension, they must have built a strong generation of partners behind them who are capable of sustaining the firm and continuing to make it successful. If the founders have operated "silo" practices for most of their careers and have not developed the next generation to succeed them, the continuing firm may be too weak to finance anything by way of benefits. The retirement of a law firm's first generation, therefore, is a pivotal point in the history of a law firm. It determines whether the firm will go on to be an institution or die off as a one-generation firm.

This is why end-of-career issues need to be resolved as early as possible in the life of the law firm. If everyone understands the expectations regarding retirement, the second generation of partners will be in a better position to deal with the issues. For example, some firms that were organized with an unfunded buyout in place have been successful in replacing the unfunded plans by setting aside a small percentage of firm income each year to finance the purchase of insurance annuities for the founders. This solution has three advantages. First, the founders are contributing to their retirements while they are still active. Second, the founders have the comfort of knowing that their retirements are prefunded. Third, the continuing firm, if it starts early enough, has a sufficiently long period of time to fund the annuities, so annual payments are more affordable. The only drawback is that the payments to purchase the annuities are not deductible for tax purposes.

The important thing to remember is that time is a critical factor. If retirement and succession planning begins soon after a firm is organized, both founders and successors have ample time and flexibility to craft a solution that works for everyone and that everyone understands. Each passing year makes it more difficult to change the plan or its funding mechanism. Waiting too long increases the risk that retirement issues will become contentious and even threaten the continued existence of the firm.

Chapter 5
WHAT IS A LAW FIRM WORTH?

Throughout their life cycles, most law firms encounter two significant events that give rise to questions about the value of the firm. The first such event is usually the first time the founding partner (or partners) seeks to admit a new equity partner. The second such event is usually the retirement or withdrawal of one or more of the firm's founders.

Before getting into the details of the many ways one might value a law firm, it is important to note that valuations involve a blend of hard data analysis and application of subjective judgments. There is no single best way to establish the value of a law firm. Most of the time it boils down to a negotiated settlement between the prospective buyer(s) and the seller(s).

Strictly speaking, a law firm is worth only what a *qualified* and *informed* buyer would pay for it. Since law firms can be owned only by lawyers (at least as of now and excluding Washington, DC), the field of *qualified* buyers is limited. An *informed* buyer would be a lawyer or law firm with intimate knowledge of the subject firm's client base, skills base, reputation, and finances. That limits the field even further. However, let us assume, for the moment, that such a buyer exists. How does the prospective buyer go about determining a fair value for the subject firm?

The first thing a buyer looks at is the "tangible net asset value" —a short-hand way of saying "excess of 'book' assets over liabilities." The kinds of things that go into this calculation are:

- cash and cash-like items;

- costs advanced to clients (i.e., "hard disbursements") (Note: In contingent-fee practices, these costs can be huge.);
- furniture, fixtures and equipment, net of depreciation;
- leasehold improvements, net of amortization;
- bank debt;
- other indebtedness, like credit lines, letters of credit, etc.; and
- unrecorded liabilities, like an obligation to pay contractual retirement benefits.

While the firm's financial statements are a useful starting point for this simple calculation, an *informed* buyer would want to question the collectibility of client costs advanced, the age and replacement value of furniture and equipment, and the remaining term of the firm's office lease, relative to the unamortized leasehold improvements. (If the lease is about to expire, will the firm have to move and abandon the leasehold improvements? If so, they have little or no value.) Remember, the buyer is looking at how these assets are going to benefit him or her, not what they originally cost.

The second major thing the buyer evaluates is the quality of unbilled and billed-but-uncollected accounts. While these assets are not recognized under the cash-basis accounting, they are very real assets, because they provide sources of cash to finance short-term operations. A buyer wants these assets as part of the deal, because if they are not available, the buyer will otherwise have to finance rent, staff salaries, etc., until work currently being done by the firm's lawyers gets collected. (Please refer to the case study in the previous chapter.)

Third and finally, there is the thorniest question of what the firm may be worth as a "going concern." This value is a function of how much cash the operation of the firm is expected to throw off for the benefit of the new owner (or owners), assuming that the former owner is no longer actively involved with the practice and is no longer being compensated. If, for example, the former owner's practice was so uniquely personal to him or her that clients would look for other counsel if that lawyer were not in the picture, the likelihood that the practice/firm would throw off any meaningful cash—over and above collection of outstanding accounts—is slim to none. Thus, any "going concern" value would be zero.

If, on the other hand, the client relationships left behind are really bonded to the firm, as opposed to the former owner, there is a "going concern" value to the new owner. How much a buyer would be willing to pay for the "going concern" value is a matter of balancing the expected cash generation with what the buyer might be able to earn from an alternative investment of similar risk.

For example, let's say an estate planning law firm is composed of one owner (partner) and one salaried lawyer (associate). The firm is expected to generate $750,000 annually in revenue. Total compensation and benefits paid to the associate amount to $150,000 per year, and all other operating expenses (secretarial salaries, rent, malpractice insurance, etc.) are $200,000 per year. Under these assumptions, the firm is expected to generate $400,000 in annual profit for its owner.

Determining the "going concern" value of the firm hinges upon whether the $400,000 annual profit exceeds the amount that one would have to pay a lawyer of comparable experience and expertise to generate clients and run the practice. If the annual profit exceeds that amount, there is a "going concern" value.

To complete this example, let's assume that the ALM Legal Intelligence's *Survey of Law Firm Economics* reports that an estate planning lawyer with comparable years of experience practicing in the same geographic area makes on average $300,000 per year. Thus, the owner of this practice is making $100,000 more per year than "market" compensation. One may assume that this differential is due to the quality of the firm's client base, its referral sources, the value of the estate plans in its will vault, fiduciary commissions for serving as trustee, or a wide range of other factors.

Under such conditions, a prospective successor to the owner might be willing to pay something more than the value of the cash assets, accounts receivable, and unbilled time to acquire the firm—provided he or she can be persuaded that whatever factors are responsible for generating this premium compensation will stay with the firm once the present owner withdraws or retires. Just how much the successor would be willing to pay depends upon what alternative investments are available to the successor and how much he or she can earn from the alternative investments. In this case, let's assume that the best alternative investment of comparable riskiness would be a publicly traded common stock that has a track record of returning 5 percent after taxes to investors in the form of capital gains and dividends.

If the successor were to invest $100,000 per year in this stock at the start of each of five successive years, he or she would expect to have $580,191 at the end of the fifth year (including the final year's payment of $100,000). Alternatively, he or she could pay a lump sum now for the stock, instead of investing annually. That lump sum (the present value of receiving $580,191 in five years' time) is $454,595. Returning to the law firm example, the successor could pay the owner of the firm $454,595 over and above the value of the law firm's other assets and still be in the same place had he or she invested in the stock.

In practical terms, this would be the maximum the successor might be prepared to pay. The actual "going concern" premium would have to be negotiated between the two parties. In cases where a premium is paid, it is done so in conjunction with a proviso that the former owner remains active in the law firm for a period of time after the date the successor purchases the firm. During that period, the former owner would be expected to introduce the successor to the firm's clients and referral sources, transfer trusteeships to the successor, and otherwise do everything possible to transition the practice to the successor.

An alternative to attempting to value the net assets and "going concern" value of the firm is to use an earnings-multiplier approach. This method of valuation is adapted from the field of securities analysis, and it is used by financial professionals to value the stock of closely held corporations. In its simplest form, the earnings of the partners, as reported on the firm's federal income tax return (Form 1065 Schedule K-1), are multiplied by the equivalent of a price-earnings (P/E) ratio.

The tricky part is determining an appropriate P/E ratio. For publicly traded companies, this number is determined by comparing published earnings per share with the company's stock price. For example, since the 1890s the S&P 500 stocks have been valued at about thirteen times earnings.

For closely held businesses, however, there is little in the way of published data. A simple approach would be to assume that the S&P 500 P/E ratio is an acceptable surrogate. But there is typically more risk inherent in an investment in a small, closely held business than in a stock for which there is a ready market. Higher risk generally means a lower P/E ratio.

Like it or not, most law firms—especially small ones—are quite risky investments. Clients are free to come and go, as are the lawyers who serve them. That's why major defections of partners from law firms can, and frequently do, result in dissolution of the firms.

The P/E ratio, or "multiplier," as it is sometimes called, is supposed to take into account the time value of money, inflation, and extra compensation for the risk the investor takes by expending present cash for an uncertain stream of potential future earnings. Alternatively stated, the multiplier reflects the amount of time the buyer is willing to wait before recovering all of his initial investment. For example, if an investor were to pay "five times earnings" for a company, he would seek to recover his initial investment in five years at the rate of 20 percent per year. If he felt the potential return was more risky, he would seek to recover his investment faster and would offer a much lower multiple, perhaps "two times earnings" (i.e., he would be willing to risk his money for only two years instead of five). In the latter case, the investor would be looking for a 50 percent annual rate of recovery.

The process of establishing an adjusted multiple is both subjective and judgmental. Because law practices are based upon individual relationships between lawyer and client, and because there is usually nothing that binds lawyer or client to the firm other than this personal relationship, it is unwise to assign a high earnings multiple in a law firm valuation. Most law firms operate with about eight or nine months of backlog (unbilled work and accounts receivable). This argues for a "rock-bottom" multiple of about 0.75 times average earnings, or about nine months' earnings.

Once a starting multiple is determined, it can be adjusted up or down to reflect the particular facts and circumstances of the firm that make it different from the standard or norm. Consideration should be given to the stability of the client base, ability of remaining lawyers to perpetuate the business, name recognition in the community served, type of practice, profitability of practice, size of firm, stability of partner group, profits reinvested into the firm by founders to fund growth, level of risk undertaken, and the like.

The process of selecting a multiple is highly subjective. What the analyst is aiming for is a number that expresses two economic variables:

1. The most likely stream of earnings that one would expect the firm to generate for its owners, expressed as a ratio to one year's historical earnings, and
2. The probability that the firm will be able to meet that target.

Let's consider an illustrative example. Assume that a law firm's three-year historical average earnings were $1,000,000, and that it normally carried nine months of backlog. Thus, at a minimum, the firm would be expected to generate $750,000 in the first year after the valuation. Translating to the multiple, that would suggest a valuation of 0.75 times earnings.

Now suppose the firm also had several new matters already booked that lawyers have not begun working on. Let's assume that they represent another six months' work. In that case, it might be reasonable to add another 0.50 points to the multiple (half a year).

Further suppose that the firm has an estate planning practice that is expected to generate an additional $500,000 of probate work over the next few years. Because the work would be spread over several years, one would discount the value of the additional fees by some factor to take into account the time value of money. Let's say that the discounted value is $450,000. Considering the probate work, an analyst might add 0.45 points to the multiple. To summarize, the base multiple now stands at 1.70 times earnings (0.75 plus 0.50 plus 0.45).

At this point, an analyst might start making subjective judgments about the probability that the firm could sustain earnings at its present level or higher long into the future. If the analyst's judgment is that the firm's most productive partners are young and have many productive years ahead of them, the analyst might increase the multiple by a few tenths of a point. If, on the other hand, the analyst has concerns about the ability of the younger lawyers in the firm to maintain the firm's client base at the same or better level of quality, the analyst might lower the multiple by a few tenths of a point.

Needless to say, this process is exceedingly unscientific and subjective. Analysts often base their analyses on years of experience with other acquisitions. Sometimes their valuations turn out to be correct and the acquiring party recovers its investment in the firm and goes on to make a profit. Other times they are wrong and the acquiring party either loses money or has to dramatically restructure the firm to protect its investment.

Looking back over my forty years of law firm consulting experience, there seems to be a consensus that a law firm's value should be in the range of one to two times earnings, typically about 1.5 times earnings. There are no empirical data studies that support this notion, other than the fact that many law firms use comparable ratios in determining pension benefits payable to retiring partners.

For now, let's consider another case study—one derived from a real-life example.

Adams & Evers, LLP

A VALUATION CASE STUDY

About eight years ago, Fred Adams and Sheila Evers founded a law firm to serve closely held businesses, their owners, and other high-net-worth individuals. They worked hard to build an excellent network of referral sources, among them accountants, insurance brokers, financial advisers, and other lawyers with whom they did not compete.

Over the years, the firm has grown to seven lawyers. Its annual fee revenues are about $4 million per year. Over the past three years, revenues have increased steadily by about 10 percent per year, and Fred and Sheila have been adding lawyers gradually to keep up with increased business.

Fred and Sheila are equal partners. They each earn about $600,000 annually, after paying the other five lawyers. The other lawyers earn a base salary, plus a bonus based upon whether they exceed targets for fees collected from their work and for fees collected from clients they introduce to the firm. There is one lawyer who, with a paralegal, handles all probate matters for the firm. He is paid a straight salary.

One of the important drivers of new business has been Seth Cain. About three years ago, Fred and Sheila decided to add litigation capability to the firm's services. They had been referring clients in need of litigation representation to Seth, who was an eighth-year lawyer with a small litigation boutique. Seth was doing a great job with the cases they referred to him. He had also made a name for himself in the community and was able to refer businesses and estate planning clients to Adams & Evers. So they decided to bring Seth over to the firm, with the hope he could become a partner in short order.

Within three years, Seth had built a $700,000 per year litigation practice staffed by Seth, an associate, and a paralegal. Between salary and bonus, Seth currently earns $200,000 per year. He also has a benefits package that is worth another $18,000 per year and "perks" (car and expense allowance) that are worth another $22,000 per year. In all, including the employer share of payroll taxes the firm pays for Seth, his job costs the firm about $250,000 per year.

The most recent year-end balance sheet for Adams & Evers is as follows:

Adams & Evers
Year-End Balance Sheet

ASSETS	
Cash on hand	$ 120,000
Client costs advances	375,000
Furniture, fixtures & equipment (net)	625,000
Total Assets	1,120,000
LIABILITIES	
Accounts payable	75,000
Bank term loan	570,000
Total Liabilities	645,000
Net Assets	$ 475,000

In addition, the firm has $850,000 in unbilled work in progress and another $650,000 in accounts receivable. The firm's accountant believes that 80 percent of the unbilled and uncollected accounts (i.e., $1,200,000) will be collected in the normal course of business.

What is the law firm of Adams & Evers worth?

To begin with, the balance sheet net assets are valued on an after-tax basis. That is, Fred and Sheila have already earned money and paid income taxes to raise the cash to pay for these assets. By comparison, the "inventory" is valued on a pretax basis. When these assets are turned into cash, they will represent revenue that will be subject to tax on Fred and Sheila's personal tax returns. So the first step is to convert the net asset values to the same tax basis.

Assuming that Fred and Sheila pay 40 percent in taxes on each additional dollar of income they make, the firm's net asset value on both bases is as follows:

Pretax Value		
Cash-basis net assets	$	475,000
Adjustment for taxes		
($475,000 divided by 60%, less $475,000)		317,000
Value of "inventory"		1,200,000
Pretax Value		1,992,000
After-tax Value		
Cash-basis net assets	$	475,000
Value of "inventory"		1,200,000
Less: Tax on "inventory" at 40%		(480,000)
After-tax Value	$	1,195,000

Using the earnings-multiplier approach is simpler. Annual earnings for both partners amount to $1,200,000. Using a multiple of 1.5 times earnings yields a pretax value of $1,800,000, or an after-tax value of $1,080,000 (60 percent of pretax value).

In conservative round numbers, it is fair to conclude that the law firm of Adams & Evers is worth $1,800,000 before taxes and $1,000,000 after taxes.

Why does tax make a difference?

If we assume that Fred and Sheila want to make Seth a 20 percent partner, he will be acquiring an asset that is worth $360,000 before taxes or $200,000 after taxes. They can offer him several ways of financing his investment in the firm. The easiest way would be to have him pay the firm $40,000 in cash each year for five years. Fred and Sheila could simply leave the cash in the firm or withdraw it in the form of a tax-free distribution.

An alternative would be for Seth to take a reduction in compensation of $72,000 each year for five years. Seth's job currently costs the firm $250,000 per year. Once he becomes a partner, the cost of his job is added into the firm's partner compensation pool, raising it from $1,200,000 to $1,450,000. His 20 percent share of the compensation pool is

$290,000 per year. If he takes out only $218,000 per year, he can finance his investment with forgone earnings, rather than having to come up with the cash to buy his interest.

This second alternative is easier on Seth, because he is "earning into" the firm. It is less beneficial to Fred and Sheila. Their 40 percent shares of the new compensation pool will be worth $580,000 each, lower by $20,000. This is offset by their halfshares of the $72,000 that Seth is forgoing, raising them back to $616,000 each.

Other alternatives exist, such as having Seth pay in, say, $20,000 per year and forgo only $36,000 per year in compensation. In any event, allowing Seth to acquire his interest by forgoing compensation is less advantageous to Fred and Sheila, but it may be the only way Seth can afford to become a partner.

Practically speaking, the process of valuing a law firm is a lot more complicated than what is described in this case study. The fundamental principles are, however, the basic building blocks of any kind of business valuation and should apply equally well in a law firm setting. Any practitioner who contemplates a transfer of his or her practice, either by selling the entire practice or by admitting a new partner, should keep these principles in mind. The practitioner should also consult his or her accountant, or a valuation expert, on how best to value the practice.

Chapter 6
TAKING CARE OF THE FOUNDERS

The previous example dealt with the creation of a new partnership interest by two founders. This chapter deals with a situation in which a "going concern" firm—i.e., one that has been in operation for several years and has already admitted a few new partners—decides it needs to work out a transition arrangement with founding partners who are ten or fifteen years away from retirement.

In such a case, the economic and interpersonal issues are a bit different from the example in which the firm is admitting its first new partner. In fact, this situation reflects a complementary, but opposite, dynamic. The issue in this case is how to transfer ownership of the firm to a new generation of active partners, as the founders contemplate a retirement and succession strategy.

The economic questions are similar to the "new partner" situation—namely, what is the firm worth and how will the succeeding partners pay for their controlling interest—but in many cases, the interpersonal issues may be more complicated. The likelihood that contemplating such a transaction might spark emotional tensions between two generations of partners is high.

On the one hand, the founders will typically view themselves as having absorbed all the entrepreneurial risk in setting up the firm, enabling it to grow, financing that growth, and creating career opportunities for those to whom they are contemplating transferring control of the firm's future. Their names are on the door, and they feel they have created the firm's "brand" that will continue long after they have gone. To them, the firm is their creation. They want it to continue to prosper, but they also want to be rewarded for taking the risks and putting in the hard work to create the firm in the first place.

By comparison, the next generation of partners probably grew up in the firm. They believe they have worked very hard to support the firm and provide healthy incomes for the founders. They may have contributed capital or may have accepted reduced compensation for acquiring their initial partnership interests. Furthermore, depending upon how historical compensation decisions have been made, they may believe that the founders have already been handsomely compensated for their role in getting the firm off the ground.

From a theoretical point of view, such a transaction is quite simple: The founders represent a group of owners who want to sell their controlling interest to a second generation of partners. The second generation represents a group of supposedly willing, competent, informed, and able buyers who seek to acquire a controlling interest in the firm. From a practical point of view, however, emotions can very often complicate the relatively simple economics of the deal.

If, for example, the second generation believes that it has already put in sufficient hard work ("sweat equity") and that the founders have controlled compensation and perks in a way that has favored them excessively, the second generation may not want to pay anything to acquire control of the firm. In such a case, the younger partners may be willing to simply sit tight and wait until the older generation retires under the existing terms of the firm's operating agreement, especially if that agreement is silent or vague with respect to retirement terms.

By contrast, the founders may believe that the operating agreement was drafted at a time when they were not contemplating retirement. They also may have introduced many clients to the firm who, over the years, have become "institutional clients" because the founders were generous in turning over client relationships to others. Furthermore, they may also expect that the firm name, which is essentially a recitation of their names, constitutes a valuable "brand" that will continue long after they have retired. Finally, they may believe that the principal reason the partners in the second generation are in a position to take over the firm is because the founders trained them and groomed them for that purpose. With these attitudes in place, the founders may be willing to sit tight and continue to control the firm, especially the compensation processes, and eventually walk away from the firm without a transition plan or even seek to merge the firm into a larger one, thereby securing the value of their partnership interests.

Irrespective of how the attitudes of the two generations are formed, they often become the negotiating positions of the two sides. When this happens, the situation can evolve into an impasse. Both sides become entrenched in emotional attitudes and neither side will give ground. The risk to the founders, however, is that the best of the second generation will simply defect to other firms, leaving the founders considerably older with no reasonable chance of rebuilding another generation of successors.

The best time to address succession issues is when the founders draft the first operating agreement. The longer founders wait to address these issues, the harder it becomes to negotiate mutually satisfactory terms. However, if the founders have been reasonably generous with those who became partners after them, and if the succeeding generations of partners see value in preserving the "brand" of the firm, a deal may be possible.

Here's another real-life example. The purpose of this case study is to illustrate how firms can devise creative ways to provide supplemental compensation to their founders. There are many different plans and possibilities, but here are the important questions to ask:

1. Is the "runway" between now and our first retirement long enough for us to accumulate a sufficient funding base?
2. Are the ages of our future beneficiaries sufficiently widely spaced to avoid bunching of retirements?
3. Can we discipline ourselves to stay with the program and consistently set money aside to fund the plan?
4. Do we feel confident in the stability of the firm and its ability to sustain moderate growth in earnings?
5. Do the rules we adopt for setting benefits create unintended consequences? For example, would our rule result in grossly overcompensating a chronically underproductive partner?

Fox, Wolfe, Sable & Lyons, LLP

A SUCCESSION CASE STUDY

The firm of Fox, Wolfe, Sable & Lyons, LLP (FWS&L) is a 16-lawyer patent and intellectual property boutique. It offers the full range of patent prosecution and litigation services, with specialties in computer software, medical devices, polymer chemistry, and generic pharmaceuticals.

The founders—the name partners—are fifty-four to fifty-seven years of age, and they set up the firm when they left a larger patent firm that has since merged into a large commercial practice law firm. In fact, the reason the four founders left their prior firm was so that they could remain an independent patent boutique.

Over the fifteen years the firm has existed, the firm's business has grown steadily at about 13 percent per year. The firm's head count has grown about 10 percent per year, so profits per partner have been very robust. Last year, the average equity partner made $650,000. The lowest-paid made $275,000 and the top-paid made just over $1 million.

The growth in the business has come in two ways: through dedicated and diligent business development efforts on the part of the founders, and through referrals from other lawyers, based upon the firm's growing reputation for delivering high-quality service at a reasonable cost.

As of today, the firm has eight equity partners and eight associates. Besides the founders, there are four other equity partners, all of whom were scientists recruited by the founders and who became lawyers through the firm's law school tuition assistance program.

The second-generation equity partners were admitted when the firm was between five and twelve years old. There are two associates who will be considered for partnership this year. Each new equity partner is required to contribute $50,000 in capital, payable at the rate of $10,000 per year for five years. Each of the new equity partners requested that this annual contribution be deducted from the year-end distribution check.

Like many patent boutiques, the firm sets equity partner compensation by formula. Collections based upon working lawyer receive 70 percent credit, collections based upon originating lawyer receive 20 percent credit, and collections based upon matter-responsible lawyer receive 10 percent credit. Most of the equity partners, including the founders, are quite good at originating business. The matter-responsible lawyer is assigned based upon the scientific discipline involved in the matter.

Early this year, the founders met with the other equity partners and expressed their desire to establish some kind of founders' benefit in the form of a deferred compensation plan. After considerable discussion, the equity partners agreed to the following broad principles:

1. While there was an agreement in principle to set up a deferred compensation plan, the younger equity partners felt that all equity partners should share, somehow, in the plan, albeit with the largest share going to the founders.
2. All agreed that equity partners should be able to claim their deferred compensation benefits at age sixty-seven, even though they may continue to work beyond age sixty-seven, and that, should a partner die before age sixty-seven, his or her estate would receive the deferred compensation benefit on the sixty-seventh anniversary of the partner's birth.
3. All agreed that an unfunded plan would not work. The founders wanted assurances that the money would be there in ten years when they would start to retire. The younger partners did not want to create a liability that would hang over the firm in the future.
4. Having seen in surveys that most firms limit aggregate retirement payments to 3 percent of distributable income, the partners agreed that they would set aside an amount equal to 3 percent of the prior year's distributable income each December and create a special restricted capital fund to finance the deferred compensation plan.
5. Since Messrs. Fox, Wolfe, Sable, and Lyons were, respectively, ages fifty-seven, fifty-six, fifty-five, and fifty-four, there appeared to be no major risk of exhausting the fund because of bunching of retirements. Since the eldest of the next generation of partners was age forty-eight, there would also be a period of years to rebuild the fund to finance the next generation's deferred compensation.
6. The partners asked the firm's chief financial officer to create a conservative forecast, using 80 percent of average net income per partner (NIPP) in the year the partner turned sixty-seven as a deferred compensation benefit for each of the founders. The remaining partners' deferred compensation benefits would be 40 percent of NIPP. Benefits would be payable in January of the year following the partner's sixty-seventh birthday.
7. To be conservative, it was assumed that the fund would be invested to earn an average of 4 percent per annum in income. To the extent fund earnings fell short of 4 percent in any one year, the firm would make up the difference. Similarly, if the fund were to earn more than 4 percent, the excess would be paid out to the firm to reimburse it. Otherwise, excess income would stay in the plan.

The CFO translated all the plan assumptions and created the following spreadsheet table:

Year	Est NIPP	Est DNI	1/1 Bal	Income	Payment	Contrib	12/31/Bal
0	650,000	5,200,000	N/A	N/A	N/A	N/A	N/A
1	682,500	5,460,000	156,000	6,240	-	163,800	326,040
2	716,625	5,733,000	326,040	13,042	-	171,990	511,072
3	752,456	6,019,650	511,072	20,443	-	180,590	712,104
4	790,079	6,320,633	712,104	28,484	-	189,619	930,207
5	829,583	6,636,664	930,207	37,208	-	199,100	1,166,515
6	871,062	6,968,497	1,166,515	46,661	-	209,055	1,422,231
7	914,615	7,316,922	1,422,231	56,889	-	219,508	1,698,628
8	960,346	7,682,768	1,698,628	67,945	-	230,483	1,997,056
9	1,008,363	8,066,907	1,997,056	79,882	-	242,007	2,318,945
10	1,058,782	8,470,252	2,318,945	92,758	-	254,108	2,665,811
11	1,111,721	8,893,765	2,665,811	106,632	(889,376)	266,813	2,149,880
12	1,167,307	9,338,453	2,149,880	85,995	(933,845)	280,154	1,582,183
13	1,225,672	9,805,376	1,582,183	63,287	(980,538)	294,161	959,094
14	1,286,956	10,295,644	959,094	38,364	(1,029,564)	308,869	276,763
15	1,351,303	10,810,427	276,763	11,071	-	324,313	612,146
16	1,418,868	11,350,948	612,146	24,486	-	340,528	977,160
17	1,489,812	11,918,495	977,160	39,086	-	357,555	1,373,802
18	1,564,303	12,514,420	1,373,802	54,952	-	375,433	1,804,186
19	1,642,518	13,140,141	1,804,186	72,167	-	394,204	2,270,558
20	1,724,644	13,797,148	2,270,558	90,822	-	413,914	2,775,295

Note: "NIPP" stands for "Net Income per Partner" and "DNI" stands for "Distributable Net Income."

Based upon this analysis, the deferred compensation plan looked like a reasonable way to reward the founders and accumulate a considerable sum to finance a similar benefit for the remaining equity partners.

Of course, a lot depends upon the assumptions. A couple of years of slow income growth or even income decline could jeopardize the plan. That said, the chief financial officer pointed out that the plan would work even if there were no growth in income; it's just that the benefits would be greatly reduced.

Poor investment performance could also hurt the plan, if the firm hadn't included a provision to guarantee a 4 percent return. The chief financial officer estimated that if average investment returns slipped below 2.75 percent over the life of the plan, absent the firm's guarantee, the plan would run a deficit in Year 14. In such an event, the partners concluded that they could negotiate a deferred payout, if necessary.

Why did this plan work? While the firm that adopted this plan several years ago was much larger than sixteen lawyers, the plan is in place today and has more than enough money in it to fund the benefits. In fact, investment returns on the plan have been so strong—even in the face of a recent recession—that the firm decided it had enough excess capital to increase the self-insured retention on its malpractice policy, which significantly cut its premiums.

The principal reasons why this plan works are as follows:

1. This is obviously a very successful law firm. However, even a firm in which the average equity partner earns, say, $250,000 could afford a parallel plan, albeit with greatly reduced benefits.
2. The founders of this firm have been and continue to be generous with their other partners. They helped with law school tuition, and they were not greedy in what they sought for a benefit.
3. The plan covers all equity partners, so no one feels like he or she is carrying an unfair load.
4. The oldest partners are young enough for the plan to accumulate considerable amounts of money. If Fox and Wolfe were, say, sixty-two years of age when the plan was adopted, it probably would not have worked.
5. Moreover, there is no major bunching of partners at the same age. If the founders were all going to trigger their benefits at the same time, there would have to be a mechanism to spread payments out over a period of time.
6. This plan works because the firm has always had a formula-based compensation system, and a nondiscretionary formula-based system generally does not allow for some classes of partner to demand premium compensation for their status within the firm. The question of a founders' benefit is treated separately from a merit-based system of compensation. This plan probably would not have succeeded in a firm with a highly or purely subjective compensation plan.
7. All the equity partners in this case, especially the founders, are highly motivated and highly productive. If this were not the case, pegging the deferred compensation benefit to average net income per partner would not be wise. In such a situation, it would be better to peg the benefit to the individual partner's formula compensation—for example, 75 percent of average of five years' most recent compensation.

Yet, for all of its good aspects, this plan is inefficient when it comes to income taxation. Contributions to the plan are not deductible, so the eight equity partners will have to pay income tax on their plan contributions at a time when their marginal tax rates are likely to be at the maximum. A possible solution to this problem would be to integrate this plan with the firm's qualified defined contribution plan so that at least part of the contributions would be deductible. That said, the accounting and discrimination testing for such an integrated plan would be very complicated.

The good news is that deferred compensation payouts under this plan are tax-free—at least under current law. Taxes on the firm income needed to fund the plan would be paid currently, as would taxes on the plan's investment returns.

For the moment, the plan still works, despite the income tax issues. However, if marginal tax rates, especially on capital gains, climb much higher, the plan might become much less attractive.

Despite the success of this plan, it must be emphasized that there is no "one-size-fits-all" nonqualified plan that will work for a large number of law firms. Such plans have to be carefully crafted and customized to the ages and retirement preferences of the individual partners. They also have to be constructed so that they will be affordable long into the future. No one can predict with certainty what a firm's net income or partner compensation will be twenty years from now.

Thus, all such plans need a cap on what percentage of firm net income can be devoted to payments to retired partners. Typically, this cap is set between 3 percent and 4 percent of net income, although some larger firms have caps that are much higher. Setting the cap too high, however, is a recipe for disaster, as many future partners may come to conclude that the amount of money going to retirees is excessive and, as a result, defect to other firms that do not have such plans.

Ideally, there should also be a provision in the plan that will keep arrearages in payments—benefits that roll over to future years—from accumulating to excessive levels. Most often, this provision simply states that if a rollover of benefits cannot be funded within, say, three years, the arrearage ceases to exist. Such a provision provides the firm protection against the possibility that active partner departures or other business downturns will result in too few partners having to shoulder the burden of a legacy liability.

Down the road, however, this plan may need to be restructured, especially if the firm adds many more partners. If future generations of partners are going to be added to the plan, care must be taken that the liability under the plan does not "run away" without anyone noticing. It would be highly advisable for the firm to re-evaluate the plan liability every two years or so to make sure it is still affordable. As we shall see in a later chapter, what looks affordable today may turn into a major liability down the road.

Chapter 7 QUALIFIED RETIREMENT PLANS

In the previous chapter, I presented a case study about a firm that set up an unfunded plan to take care of its founders and considered why the particular aspects of the plan made the plan affordable—at least in the near term. Yet, the plan was not very efficient from a tax perspective. At this point it is useful to review more tax-efficient options.

Under IRS and ERISA regulations, it is possible for a law firm to adopt a limited retirement plan for its partners and employees under which contributions to the plan are tax deductible and under which taxes on plan earnings are deferred until benefits are paid out. These types of plans are generally referred to as "qualified plans." They must cover all employees, must not favor so-called highly paid participants over other classes of employees, and must pass annual discrimination tests.

When considering the establishment of a retirement plan for a law firm, qualified plans should be at the top of the list. They provide for current funding, and the funding payments are deductible for tax purposes. Even though these plans involve incurring some costs to set up and maintain, the tax advantages available to the law firm's partners far outweigh the costs and regulatory compliance that go along with them. Given enough time and a well-thought-out investment strategy, partners can amass substantial retirement assets on a tax-deferred basis.

A full examination of all the different options available—and their funding and testing ramifications—would require a much more extensive text than is contemplated by this book. This chapter is based upon personal experience and general familiarity with qualified retirement plans. No law firm should attempt to adopt a qualified retirement plan without seeking advice of financial planning and tax experts. However, it is worth providing an overview of qualified plans in order to consider how they may be best integrated into retirement and succession plans of law firms.

Virtually all plan designs require answering a series of questions, namely the following:

1. How are retirement benefits to be calculated?
2. Through what mechanism will they be funded?
3. What happens when people change jobs?
4. Who is responsible for making decisions regarding the investment of plan funds?
5. Who bears the risk of market fluctuations in the prices of fund investments?
6. What restrictions and regulations apply with respect to plan contributions, plan withdrawals, loans against plan balances, etc.?

As for the calculation of benefits, there are generally two common plan types—defined-benefit plans and defined-contribution plans. (There is a bit of a hybrid called a cash balance plan, but I'll leave the description of that type of plan to the experts.)

The defined-benefit plan calculates retirement benefits as a percentage of the employee's or partner's preretirement compensation. (Please refer to Chapter 2 that traces the history of law firm retirement plans.) These plans work like Social Security—a classic example of a defined-benefit plan. Retirement benefits become available when one retires, and they continue in the form of a monthly payment for the retiree's lifetime, occasionally with a reduced benefit for a surviving spouse, but this is rare in today's world.

By contrast, in a defined-contribution plan, the individual makes contributions, not the sponsoring firm. Often, but not always, plan sponsors make matching contributions on behalf of employees to encourage them to participate in the plan. Generally speaking, the more employees participate in such plans, the easier it is to pass discrimination and other tests.

In defined-benefit plans, employers or partnerships are responsible for making sufficient contributions each year so that the assets in the plan fund (including interest, dividends, and capital gains) will be sufficient to cover payment of the contractual obligations to retirees. There are no individual fund balances, only one big pool of assets that will be used to satisfy future obligations. Consequently, it is very important for the sponsoring firm to invest this pool of assets prudently, lest the plan assets not grow at a pace sufficient to meet the eventual obligations.

When an employee changes jobs, the issue of portability looms to the fore. If the employee has met the vesting requirements for the defined-contribution plan, he or she simply rolls over the balance of the account to a new retirement trust account set up for that purpose. With a defined-benefit plan, what typically happens is that the employee's stake in the retirement benefit is frozen at an amount equal to the present value of the obligation that will be due him or her upon retirement. The employee cannot normally withdraw the funds allocated for his or her defined-benefit plan because the assets are commingled with the assets needed to fund all other plan participants' benefits. Thus, defined-benefit plans are decidedly nonportable when one changes jobs.

In a defined-benefit plan, the employer appoints a board of trustees to oversee the investment of plan assets, usually under the guidance of a professional investment adviser. The board makes all decisions regarding investments, and the board is accountable to plan participants for ensuring that there will be sufficient funds available to pay benefits when they come due. Note that this is a very big fiduciary responsibility of the plan sponsor (employer).

Under federal regulations, such plans must pay annual premiums to the Pension Benefit Guarantee Corporation (PBGC)—a government entity that insures pension obligations in the case of an asset shortfall. In addition, the sponsor must hire an actuary each year to compute the present value of accrued benefits (PVAB) owed by the plan and compare the value of that obligation with the value of the assets currently in the pension fund. If there is a shortfall, the sponsor must make additional contributions to make up the difference, usually over a period of years, until the assets are sufficient to cover most of the PVAB.

Needless to say, the costs associated with maintaining a qualified defined-benefit plan are greater than those associated with defined-contribution plans. Under the latter, no premiums are due the PBGC, and the plan does not have to have an annual actuarial evaluation.

In contrast, investment choices in the defined-contribution plan are the responsibility of the plan participant. The plan sponsor has to appoint a board of trustees, but its job is limited to selecting and maintaining a menu of options into which participants may choose to invest their contributions. Most law firm plans also offer provisions that let participants self-direct their funds to investment choices not listed in the standard investment options of the plan. The responsibility of the trustees in this case is to manage the quality of the core funds and weed out those that don't perform according to the trustees' guidelines.

As for market fluctuations, in a defined-benefit plan the employer/sponsor must absorb all the risk, subject to some insurance coverage through the PBGC. Hence, employers are increasingly wary of sponsoring such plans unless they are really good at picking investments. In a defined-contribution plan, the employee absorbs all market risk. There are no safeguards. If the employee mismanages his or her own investments, too bad.

Since assets are commingled in a defined-benefit plan, participants are not allowed to withdraw assets (other than to receive pension benefits), nor are they allowed to borrow against the value of pension benefits that will eventually be due them. Participants in defined-contribution plans may, after paying a penalty and accrued taxes, withdraw funds prior to retiring. Moreover, they can also borrow from their accounts without paying a penalty. Restrictions do apply, however.

The general rule with qualified plans is that they should not discriminate in favor of "highly paid employees." That means firm contributions made on behalf of partners must be balanced against firm contributions made on behalf of all other "non–highly paid" employees. Generally, associates fall under the category of "highly paid employees," but they are less likely to stick around long enough to vest meaningfully in any plan benefits. Law firms often avoid the discrimination issue by setting up two separate plans—a defined-contribution plan, with or without an employer match, that just covers associates, and a separate defined-benefit or profit-sharing plan that covers partners and all other nonlawyer employees.

Vesting rules can also affect how these plans work. In most defined-contribution plans, employees become eligible to make contributions after about one year of employment. By comparison, defined-benefit plans often require many years of employment service and/or years of seniority as a partner to qualify for full benefits.

This has been a very high-level survey of retirement plan options. For a more thorough treatment, please refer to Chapter 4.31 of *Best Practices in Legal Management: A Comprehensive Guide* (New York State Bar Association 2010). Obviously, designing a qualified plan for a law firm is a complex task that requires advice from accountants, financial planners, and pension specialists. As with some of the nonqualified plans discussed previously, the success of any plan depends a lot on the level of benefits and the age distribution of the partners. When designing any plan, it is always best to create a computer-based model of the estimated paid benefits and the contributions needed to fund them.

Qualified plans can be very useful tools for partially funding nonqualified retirement benefits, and many law firms use them for this purpose. For example, in a previous chapter, we presented a case study that analyzed a deferred compensation plan that was funded by the firm by making an annual contribution of 3 percent of new distributable income. In that example, the firm was simply setting aside funds from current earnings, and the partners were paying income tax on 100 percent of their shares of income but only receiving 97 percent of the income in cash. In addition, they also had to pay income tax on the annual earnings of the retirement fund.

A more efficient way to fund the retirement benefits from a tax point of view would have been to set up a cash balance plan or profit-sharing plan, whereby the firm would contribute, say, 4.5 percent of income each year to individual accounts of the four partners. Under this kind of qualified plan, the firm—and the partners—would get a tax deduction for the annual contributions, and the annual income of the plan would not be subject to tax until benefits are paid.

Regulations governing qualified retirement plans are very complicated. Suffice it to say that no law firm should attempt to set up such a plan without expert advice from ERISA lawyers and independent financial planners. My only purpose for including a limited discussion of such plans in this book is to make readers aware of the fact that such choices exist.

Chapter 8

MAKING UNAFFORDABLE PLANS GO AWAY

Chapter 6 dealt with designing unfunded, *nonqualified* defined-benefit retirement plans that have a chance of lasting for a considerable number of years. Eventually, however, even the best of such plans can become unaffordable. Also, these plans often get in the way of successful law firm merger and acquisition transactions. Firms that do not have such plans generally do not want to assume the liabilities of another firm with which they are contemplating a merger. The retirement plan, quite simply, becomes a "poison pill" that interferes with the execution of what might otherwise be a successful strategic combination.

Even *qualified* defined-benefit pension plans can become unaffordable. Defined-benefit plans are not like retirement savings plans. Essentially, they constitute a promise to pay a certain level of benefits upon retirement. Employers make annual contributions to the plan that are intended to grow in value to a point where the plan assets are great enough to fund the future benefits when they come due. The challenges of managing such plans are:

1. investing plan assets so that the assets will increase in value over time; and
2. deciding how much must be contributed each year to ultimately fund the eventual payment of benefits, taking into account the expected return derived from investing the plan assets.

Either or both of two bad things can happen. Either the annual contributions are insufficient to fund the plan, or the plan investors are wrong about their expectations as to the investment earnings on the assets in the plan. When these bad things happen, such plans can become underfunded which means the present value of the promised benefit payments far exceeds the value of the assets invested in the plans.

Testing whether a defined-benefit plan is adequately funded is a job of highly trained and highly skilled actuaries. Such testing must also be performed under complex rules promulgated by the PBGC which insures pension plans in much the same way that the Federal Deposit Insurance Corporation (FDIC) insures bank deposits.

In recent years, many qualified defined-benefit pension plans have become underfunded, because either the plan sponsors have not made sufficient annual contributions to the plans or the actual return on the invested assets has fallen well below expectations. So even these highly regulated plans can become unaffordable because of underfunding. For that reason, many law firms are trying to find ways to terminate underfunded defined-benefit plans.

In the case of most nonqualified plans—as adopted by law firms—future benefits are expected to be funded out of the future earnings of the firm, when the obligations come due. On the surface, this may seem a reasonable proposition. Today's partners do not have to set aside any money to fund the plan. Tomorrow's partners will fund the plan when today's partners decide to retire. Each succeeding generation of partners, therefore, funds the retirement benefits paid to the preceding generation.

Generally, this scheme works until a particular generation of partners decides it does not want to fund retirement benefits that will be paid to older generations who no longer create value for the firm. Alternatively, the pending liability of retirement promises becomes an obstacle when the law firm with the plan tries to merge with another firm that does not have a similar plan—or its ensuing liability.

Making unfunded or underfunded plans go away is a challenging task. First, the amount of benefits payable under the plan must be frozen. So if the plan promises to pay a certain percentage of terminal compensation to a retiree, subject to plan vesting rules, one has to calculate what that benefit is worth in today's dollars and substitute that present value for the promise to pay a future benefit.

Second, a plan must be put in place to eventually pay the frozen benefits. This often involves setting aside some portion of current earnings to be used to pay the frozen benefits when the partner eventually does retire. A nonqualified plan can be restructured to reduce payouts, grandfather some older partners, and eliminate the plan for all others.

Alternatively, in the case of nonqualified unfunded plans, some partners may be persuaded to voluntarily forgo their retirement entitlements. This is not totally without precedent. I have seen several cases in which senior law firm partners have agreed to forgo benefits in exchange for compensation guarantees while they still remain active partners. Practically speaking, however, getting partners to voluntarily give up benefits is very difficult. Furthermore, the liability to pay those partners who are already retired and receiving benefits is a real contractual liability that must be satisfied, unless the law firm is in bankruptcy. The same is true for any nonpartner employees who might be covered by a qualified plan.

If the plan is a qualified defined-benefit plan, its termination must be accomplished within rules established by the IRS, ERISA, and the PBGC. It is a very complex and highly technical process that is outside the intended scope of this book. Suffice it to say, terminating any qualified plan should not be attempted without the guidance and counsel of expert lawyers, actuaries, and accountants.

Nonqualified plans are contractual in nature and not regulated by governmental agencies. Thus, they can be restructured and/or terminated by negotiating new terms with the participants. Some of the various options and techniques are probably better understood if we consider another case study.

Holmes, Watson & Moriarty, LLP

THE CASE OF THE DISAPPEARING PLAN

About twenty-five years ago, Messrs. Holmes, Watson, and Moriarty joined forces to found a new law firm in Washington, DC. The three lawyers were experts in handling matters involving federal regulation of transportation, telecommunications, and broadcasting. They also attracted a fourth lawyer, Susan Spade, who started as a nonequity partner.

About four years after they founded the firm, they decided to make Susan Spade an equity partner. By this time, the firm had grown to eight lawyers and had become very profitable.

At the same time, they decided to formalize their partnership by drafting and adopting a partnership agreement. That agreement included a contractual retirement arrangement that required partners to retire at the end of the calendar year in which they reached the age of sixty-five. Each retiring partner was entitled to receive a ten-year pension. The annual payment would be equal to one-tenth of the partner's average final three years of compensation, multiplied by a factor of 1.5.

The three founders and Susan Spade were immediately fully vested in the retirement plan. Succeeding generations of partners would vest gradually over a ten-year period, starting at 10 percent vesting at age forty-six and continuing to increase by ten percentage points per year until they became 100 percent vested at age fifty-five.

To protect the firm, the plan provided that payments to retired partners in any year may not exceed 4 percent of firm operating income, basically firm net income before deducting payments to retired partners. To date, retiree payments have never hit the cap.

The founders also agreed to a compensation system that was largely a seniority-driven, lockstep system, with occasional bonuses for business origination. The compensation for newer partners advanced at a faster rate than for the older partners. Eventually, the base compensation percentage of a partner would reach a plateau, and further increases in compensation would have to come from the business origination bonus or from overall increases in the net income of the firm.

Over the years, the business of the firm grew to encompass representation of corporate clients in very complex matters involving a wide range of federal administrative regulation. As of the end of last year, the firm had fourteen active equity partners and about thirty associates and nonlawyer regulatory consultants. Messrs. Holmes and Watson both retired at age sixty-five and later died, at ages seventy-eight and eighty-one, respectively. Mr. Moriarty and three other partners all retired at age sixty-five and are receiving pension payments under the retirement plan.

Average partner compensation over the past three years has been $575,000, with the lowest-compensated partner making $250,000 and the highest making $900,000 per year. Over the course of the years, average partner income has grown steadily at about 5 percent per year—some years higher, some lower.

Last June, the firm was approached by a large national law firm interested in merging with Holmes, Watson & Moriarty. Discussions broke off, however, when the larger firm learned of HWM's unfunded pension plan. The other firm had abandoned its unfunded pension plan several years ago and was not interested in taking on another unfunded liability.

The failed merger discussions and the concerns over the pension liability led HWM's management to retain a consulting firm to advise them on what to do, if anything, about the retirement plan liability. The consultants reviewed the firm's financial history and the equity partners' historical compensation. Allowing for the continuation of a steady 5 percent overall growth in earnings, they estimated what each equity partner would be earning at age sixty-five. To do this, they had to allow for slightly faster compensation growth for the younger partners to reflect the fact that they would be moving up the lockstep tiers.

Holmes, Watson & Moriarty, LLP
Analysis of Retirement Plan Liability

				Retirees		Active Partners					
Partner	Status	Age	% Vested	Annual Vested Benefit	Number of Payments Remaining	Years to Age 65	Current 3-Yr Avg Comp	Est Annual Comp Growth Rate	Est Annual Comp at Age 65	Annual Vested Benefit	Pres Val of Vested Benefit
Holmes	Deceased		0%	-							-
Watson	Deceased		0%	-							-
Moriarty	Retired	70	100%	90,000	5						412,174
Spade	Retired	69	100%	75,000	6						406,289
Cross	Retired	65	100%	75,000	10						639,765
Marple	Retired	65	100%	75,000	10						639,765
Poirot	Active	62	100%			3	900,000	5%	1,041,863	156,279	1,219,971
Bobbsey	Active	55	100%			10	900,000	5%	1,466,005	219,901	1,395,770
Swift	Active	53	70%			12	900,000	5%	1,616,271	242,441	1,450,501
Jones	Active	51	60%			14	900,000	5%	1,781,938	267,291	1,507,378
Reacher	Active	50	50%			15	600,000	6%	1,437,935	215,690	1,180,950
Corey	Active	49	40%			16	575,000	6%	1,460,702	219,105	1,164,707
Sutter	Active	48	30%			17	550,000	6%	1,481,025	222,154	1,146,516
Rapp	Active	48	30%			17	550,000	6%	1,481,025	222,154	1,146,516
Robicheaux	Active	46	10%			19	500,000	6%	1,512,800	226,920	1,103,887
Lebowsky	Active	45	0%			20	450,000	7%	1,741,358	261,204	1,233,656
Solchak	Active	40	0%			25	350,000	7%	1,899,601	284,940	1,160,867
Potter	Active	36	0%			29	275,000	7%	1,956,421	293,463	1,062,266
Weasley	Active	35	0%			30	250,000	7%	1,903,064	285,460	1,003,199
Granger	Active	35	0%			30	250,000	7%	1,903,064	285,460	1,003,199

Firm Net Income	7,950,000	**Present Value of Plan Liability**	18,877,378
Payments to Retired Partners	315,000	**Present Value per Active Partner**	1,348,384
Firm Operating Income	8,265,000		
Payments as % Op Inc	3.81%		

The next step was to use the estimated compensation at age sixty-five to determine the likely annual retirement payment to each partner for each of the ten years after age sixty-five ("Annual Vested Benefit"). As per the plan, the benefit is one tenth of 1.5 times compensation at age sixty-five. It was also assumed that all current partners would eventually become fully vested in the plan.

The final step was to estimate how much money the firm would have to invest at that point in thirty-year U.S. Treasury bonds, which were earning about 3 percent interest, to pay each current equity partner his or her retirement benefits when they come due. This estimate is called the "Present Value of Vested Benefit" in the table. Adding all the present values for the active partners set the present value of plan liability at roughly $18.9 million, or about $1.3 million per active equity partner.

This table was troubling to most of the younger partners. As Roberta Weasley pointed out, "We're being asked to assume an average liability of $1.3 million, when the present value of our vested benefit is barely over $1 million! In fact, only three partners are going to see benefits that exceed the average liability! That's not a good thing."

The consultants also projected the total of the annual payment that would have to be made each year to take care of all of the existing plan participants. The goal was to estimate how much operating income the firm would have to earn in each of the next forty years to avoid hitting the 4 percent cap.

The following table summarizes the consultants' analysis through the next twenty-two years until the plan reaches the highest annual liability and the greatest number of retirees.

Looking at the next three years, the consultants concluded that the plan's cap would not come into play, because only the four already-retired partners would be collecting benefits, and their benefits are relatively modest.

The first bunching issue will occur in four years, when Poirot retires. Total payment due in that year will be $471,279. For the plan payments to avoid the 4 percent cap, operating income in that year would have to be $11.8 million ($471,279 divided by 4 percent). To reach that level, the firm's operating income would have to grow at an annual rate of nearly 11 percent, more than double its historical rate of growth. If that does not happen, retiree benefit payments would have to be spread over multiple years.

The good news is, after five years, the aggregate payments drop to within the "normal" range because, instead of five partners receiving benefits, there will be only three, and eventually only two. However, the number of retirees rises fairly rapidly after fifteen years, topping out at eight partners. At this point the annual liability will rise to about $1.9 million and the firm's operating income will have to be roughly $47 million. This would require an annual growth rate in operating income of more than 9 percent.

Operating Income Required to Fund Existing Plan Participants

Year	Plan Payments	Income Required	Number of Retirees
1	315,000	7,875,000	4
2	315,000	7,875,000	4
3	315,000	7,875,000	4
4	471,279	11,781,984	5
5	471,279	11,781,984	5
6	381,279	9,531,984	4
7	306,279	7,656,984	3
8	306,279	7,656,984	3
9	306,279	7,656,984	3
10	306,279	7,656,984	3
11	376,180	9,404,504	2
12	376,180	9,404,504	2
13	618,621	15,465,519	3
14	462,341	11,558,534	2
15	729,632	18,240,804	3
16	945,322	23,633,060	4
17	1,164,428	29,110,693	5
18	1,608,735	40,218,381	7
19	1,608,735	40,218,381	7
20	1,835,655	45,891,380	8
21	1,876,958	46,923,953	8
22	1,876,958	46,923,953	8

It was the consultants' conclusion that the firm cannot afford the plan as it is presently structured, because of the problem posed by bunching of retirements. The younger partners were also upset by the size of the looming liability they would have to carry. To be sure, another generation of partners may come along behind them and help share the burden, but they would eventually qualify for the plan and sadd to the liability.

The consultants offered several possibilities as to what to do about the plan. Their first recommendation was to not allow any additional partners to participate in the plan. This would help keep the liability from growing. Successor generations would essentially have to pay out the plan for the presently active partners and self-fund their own retirements through a qualified defined-contribution plan. The partners agreed that this had to be done, because the plan, as it stands, is unaffordable.

The other options proposed by the consultants were the following:

1. Keep the plan in place, as is, and live with the fact that, because of the 4 percent cap, the annual benefits would have to be spread over a longer period. Some of the younger partners objected to this suggestion because it would be likely that the older partners would get paid out in the relatively near term and the younger partners might never collect their full benefits.
2. At the other extreme, retain the plan only for those who are currently retired and terminate the plan for everyone else. Needless to say, Poirot was not happy with this suggestion.
3. Limit the annual retirement benefit to one-tenth of a single year's compensation instead of one-tenth of 1.5 times compensation. Poirot grumbled, but said he could go along with this change. He also understood that he probably would be out-voted if he forced a partnership vote on the issue.
4. Freeze the liabilities for each partner at a multiple of current compensation, instead of compensation at age sixty-five. Under this option, everyone would collect something beginning at age sixty-five, but the younger partners' benefits would be quite small.
5. Freeze the vesting percentages in place so that, for example, the five youngest partners would get nothing because they would cease to vest. Robicheaux would get 10 percent of the benefit, and so on up the vesting schedule.

The consultants also suggested that some combination of options 3, 4, and 5 might work. The firm asked the consultants to run additional analyses based upon options 3, 4, and 5.

Option 3 (lowering the multiple), alone, did little to ease the two bunching issues. HWM would still need better than 7 percent growth in operating income in the near and long term to avoid hitting the cap. Similarly, option 4 (basing benefit upon current compensation) addressed the long-term bunching issue (4.5 percent required growth) but did little to address the near-term bunching issue (9.3 percent required growth). Option 5 (applying current vesting percentages) easily solved the long-term bunching issue by taking five partners out of the plan and substantially reducing benefits for many others. It did nothing to solve the near-term issue because Poirot and the other four retirees are still 100 percent vested.

In the end, a negotiated solution was reached. All partners agreed to lower the earnings multiple to 1.0 and to freeze the benefit based upon current earnings. As a special concession, Poirot agreed to reduce his benefit to $75,000, but the firm would increase the number of years of payout from ten to fourteen to compensate for inflation and the time value of money. This reduced the near-term bunching issue to a point where only 5.5 percent growth in operating income was required to keep the plan from hitting the cap. (See the following tables.)

Holmes Watson & Moriarty, LLP
Analysis of Retirement Plan Liability
Option 6: Reduce Compensation Multiple to 1.0, Base Benefit on Current Compensation and Poirot Exception

				Retirees		Active Partners					
Partner	Status	Age	% Vested	Annual Vested Benefit	Number of Payments Remaining	Years to Age 65	Current 3-yr Avg Comp	Est Annual Comp Growth Rate	Est Annual Comp at Age 65	Annual Vested Benefit	Pres Val of Vested Benefit
Holmes	Deceased		0%	-							-
Watson	Deceased		0%	-							-
Moriarty	Retired	70	100%	90,000	5						412,174
Spade	Retired	69	100%	75,000	6						406,289
Cross	Retired	65	100%	75,000	10						639,765
Marple	Retired	65	100%	75,000	10						639,765
Poirot	Active	62	100%			3	900,000	5%	1,041,863	75,000	585,476
Bobbsey	Active	55	100%			10	900,000	5%	1,466,005	90,000	571,254
Swift	Active	53	70%			12	900,000	5%	1,616,271	90,000	538,462
Jones	Active	51	60%			14	900,000	5%	1,781,938	90,000	507,552
Reacher	Active	50	50%			15	600,000	6%	1,437,935	60,000	328,513
Corey	Active	49	40%			16	575,000	6%	1,460,702	57,500	305,655
Sutter	Active	48	30%			17	550,000	6%	1,481,025	55,000	283,850
Rapp	Active	48	30%			17	550,000	6%	1,481,025	55,000	283,850
Robicheaux	Active	46	10%			19	500,000	6%	1,512,800	50,000	243,233
Lebowsky	Active	45	0%			20	450,000	7%	1,741,358	45,000	212,533
Solchak	Active	40	0%			25	350,000	7%	1,899,601	35,000	142,593
Potter	Active	36	0%			29	275,000	7%	1,956,421	27,500	99,543
Weasley	Active	35	0%			30	250,000	7%	1,903,064	25,000	87,858
Granger	Active	35	0%			30	250,000	7%	1,903,064	25,000	87,858

Note: Poirot's buyout term was increased to 14 years

Firm Net Income	7,950,000
Payments to Retired Partners	315,000
Firm Operating Income	8,265,000
Payments as % Op Inc	3.8%

Present Value of Plan Liability	6,376,225
Present Value per Active Partner	455,445

Year	Plan Payments	Income Required	Number of Retirees
1	315,000	7,875,000	4
2	315,000	7,875,000	4
3	315,000	7,875,000	4
4	390,000	9,750,000	5
5	390,000	9,750,000	5
6	300,000	7,500,000	4
7	225,000	5,625,000	3
8	225,000	5,625,000	3
9	225,000	5,625,000	3
10	225,000	5,625,000	3
11	165,000	4,125,000	2
12	165,000	4,125,000	2
13	255,000	6,375,000	3
14	255,000	6,375,000	3
15	345,000	8,625,000	4
16	405,000	10,125,000	5
17	462,500	11,562,500	6
18	497,500	12,437,500	7
19	497,500	12,437,500	7
20	547,500	13,687,500	8
21	502,500	12,562,500	8
22	502,500	12,562,500	8

The younger partners were supportive of the agreement because they would still receive some benefit, albeit drastically reduced, rather than being completely excluded from the plan.

This solution, of course, only froze the plan in place. It did not eliminate it. That required a second negotiated solution.

If the firm were to continue without a merger, the partners believed they could live with the plan as structured, because no future partners would be added to the plan. On the other hand, liability would still pose a potential problem with a merger, if the merger partner objected to the plan.

The partners discussed a few options with the consultants but eventually agreed that, if a merger with another firm offered a compelling strategic opportunity, they would agree to abandon the plan altogether, as part of the merger terms. Only the four retirees and Poirot would receive plan benefits.

The purpose of this case study is to illustrate some of the problems firms encounter with unfunded pension obligations. It also illustrates how plan elements can be tweaked to freeze the plan in place, while not disenfranchising those who are merely a few years away from retirement.

Here are some further observations:

1. This is a perfect example of the law of unintended consequences. The plan was put in place many years ago when the firm was small and just starting out. Holmes, Watson, and Moriarty had no way of knowing just how successful their firm would become and how many partners would subsequently become plan participants. The number of participants, the growth in earnings—and resulting pension obligations—and the bunching of ages all conspired to jeopardize the plan and make it an obstacle to a strategic merger.
2. Plans like this one require firms to make judgments based upon estimates of what might happen twenty, thirty, or forty years in the future. Who among us can estimate with clarity what inflation and interest rates will be decades from now? Who can forecast law firm earnings? Who can say how many partners will be admitted and will become vested in the plan? Severely restricted plans can survive, if their purpose is merely to provide a buyout for founders and "a little something" for future generations of partners.
3. Fixing unaffordable plans involves more than just data analysis. Success comes with the skill and art of negotiating compromises. Generally, there are at least three interest groups whose needs and feelings must be addressed. **First,** there are those, like Poirot, who are very close to retirement, who have included firm retirement benefits in their personal retirement plans, and who are very reluctant to give up what they deem to be an earned entitlement.

   Second, there are the youngest partners, who have long careers ahead of them and who have mobility on their side. These partners are the future of the firm, and firm leaders need to be careful not to enact policies that encourage them to move to other firms.

   Finally, there are the middle partners, who are in their most productive years and probably their years of highest compensation. They are needed to develop business, delegate and supervise matters, and manage the firm. They also generally have a sufficient number of productive years ahead of them to organize their personal financial plans and adjust for changes in firm retirement policies.

This case study illustrates how all three interest groups gave up potential benefits for the good of the firm. Because everyone compromised, a workable solution was reached. Everyone participated in the discussions and put opinions and concerns on the table. If the leaders of the firm had attempted to cram a solution down the throats of any of the interest groups, there never would have been enough votes to implement a solution.

4. Forty years ago, law firm defined-benefit plans were very popular. They were designed around the kinds of plans adopted by corporate America in the 1950s to satisfy union demands. Unfortunately, corporate America's plans, and their private-sector cousins, have gotten into trouble because employers, eager to manage current earnings by keeping current labor costs down, fattened plan benefits to substitute for granting higher wage increases. They further managed earnings by funding plan contributions at the lowest permissible level. The results of these tactics are now coming home to roost. Plan benefits are huge, and recent poor investment returns have further weakened the asset pools that are supposed to fund the plans.

   The same is now happening to qualified defined-benefit plans at law firms. The nonqualified plans, since they lack any kind of funding base, are in even worse shape.

These days, corporate America and the public sector are trying to limit membership in the traditional plans and move new employees into defined-contribution plans. Many law firms are following suit with their unfunded plans. Eventually, many of these plans will disappear and be replaced by defined-contribution plans that may involve some current retirement funding through shared captive investment pools in which partners can collectively invest money that they do not need for living purposes. For example, some firms' office space is owned either by the firm or by a private investment partnership of the partners.

Whatever vehicles are used for law firm retirement planning, they will most often involve some way to currently fund any benefits. The future is simply too unpredictable for the old unfunded-plan approach to work.

Chapter 9

RETIREMENT—MANDATORY OR OPTIONAL?

While businesses can no longer unilaterally require aging employees to retire, many law firms still have policies that force partners to retire or at least "step out of equity" at a certain age. The argument is that partners are owners of the business and not employees, placing them outside the reach of laws that prohibit employment discrimination based upon age.

Such policies came into practice in the 1950s, as many law firms formalized partnership agreements along the lines of the ABA Model Partnership Agreement. Mandatory retirement was a natural extension of seniority-driven lockstep compensation systems. New partners would climb the ladder to parity with other partners, and older partners would scale down—usually starting at age sixty-five—until they retired at age seventy.

The policy also went hand in hand with a nonqualified, unfunded retirement plan. Such plans typically paid a retired partner an annual lifetime pension equal to 20 to 25 percent of the average of his highest five years of compensation. Often, the plan also provided for a ten-year surviving-spouse benefit and lifetime health insurance coverage for the retired partner and his spouse.

The rationale expressed for adopting such policies included:

1. to get older partners (and firm founders) into retirement to make room for younger partners;

2. to reflect expected declining productivity and contribution of partners as they age, without doing damage to the lockstep compensation system;
3. to force older partners to turn over control of client relationships to the firm;
4. to discourage partners from "hanging around" because they had not provided for their own retirements; and
5. to avoid the unpleasant task of having to tell an aging senior that he no longer has a place at the firm.

Within the context of mid-twentieth-century law practice, mandatory retirement policies were not necessarily a bad thing. Law firms were much smaller than they are today. Many younger lawyers had delayed their careers to serve in World War II and needed opportunities to catch up. Defined-benefit pension plans—a relatively new idea—were being adopted by major corporations, which had the effect of encouraging workers to retire. Finally, most people simply didn't live much beyond age sixty-five.

A lot has changed since the 1950s and 1960s. Law firms have grown at near exponential rates, filling their partnership ranks with thousands of baby boomers. The changing demographics have made unfunded defined-benefit plans nonsustainable. Old defined-benefit plans have been replaced by pay-as-you-go defined-contribution plans. Lockstep has given way to merit-based compensation. With increasing free agency of partners, control of client relationships has become a major leverage point in compensation deliberations. Clients have also shifted their loyalties from "the firm" to individual lawyers. People are living longer and may need to work longer to fund eventual retirement.

As some law firms adopted the corporate form of organization or converted to limited liability companies (LLCs) or professional limited liability companies (PLLCs), "partners" have become "shareholders" and "members," who are also employees of the firm. Once owners have attained employee status, mandatory retirement policies become open to legal challenge as age discriminatory. In fact, mandatory retirement policies of large law firms that still operate as partnerships are being challenged in the courts both in the United States and elsewhere. For a thorough treatment of this topic in the United States, please see David B. Wilkins's article "Partner, Shmartner! EEOC v. Sidley Austin Brown & Wood" in the *Harvard Law Review* (Wilkins 2007). The EEOC announcement of the resolution of its case can be found on its website: www.eeoc.gov/eeoc/newsroom/release/10-5-07.cfm.

Until this case, law partnerships insisted that their mandatory retirement policies were valid because, as true business owners, their partners were not subject to employment regulations. The argument was based upon the fact that partners share pro rata in the profits and losses of the law firm and thus, are fully "at risk." They also contribute capital to the firm and have a say in the management of the firm. Over the years, however, many firms grow so big that management committees begin making all the decisions, including setting partner compensation and deciding on partnership admissions. The more removed partners are from decision-making, the easier it is to classify them as employees.

It is probably safe to conclude that mandatory retirement within the law partnership context will eventually fall to a successful legal challenge. Historically, partners were unlikely to challenge mandatory retirement, mainly because the golden parachutes offered were so rich. Today's law partners are being asked to bear the principal weight of funding their own retirements. For those who find themselves underfunded at, say, age sixty-seven, there will be an incentive to challenge a policy that forces them to retire at age seventy. At some point, the distinction between "partner" and "employee" becomes a matter of semantics, and courts will extend antidiscrimination protection to "partners" as a matter of public policy. Bottom line, while mandatory retirement policies may have some utility, they will become increasingly harder to defend.

How, then, are law firms to encourage practice succession, deal with underperforming elders, make room for rising stars, institutionalize client relationships, etc.? These are not necessarily age-related issues. They are performance-related issues. For starters, firms can do a better job of defining and communicating criteria for attaining and sustaining equity status. Partners—of any age—who don't meet the criteria can be dealt with through compensation and/or conversion to nonequity status. Client succession and development of "next-generation" partners can be included as performance criteria. Whatever the solution, law firms will have to manage their businesses more directly and not rely on blanket policies to deal with performance issues.

In January 2007, the New York State Bar Association's Special Committee on Age Discrimination in the Profession issued its "Report and Recommendations on Mandatory Retirement Practices in the Profession." The scope of the committee's mission was to study a number of policies and practices widely used by law firms in New York State.

They included

- hiring and firing practices;
- mandatory retirement;
- "up-or-out" policies;
- age-based hierarchical staffing of cases;
- "of counsel" retention policies;
- setting hourly rates;
- noncompete clauses, especially when combined with mandatory retirement policies
- other age-discriminatory policies.

While the committee's mission had a broad scope, its attention was focused primarily on mandatory retirement practices. The committee concluded as follows:

> ... mandatory retirement—requiring a partner to leave the firm upon reaching an arbitrary age—is not an acceptable practice. Modern experience demonstrates that this practice is both unwarranted and unwise. A lawyer's age, standing alone, is not an appropriate criterion for determining professional capacity or employment status.

Thus, while the committee did pay some deference to the voluntary, contractual nature of agreements among law partners, it basically concluded that age-based retirement policies run counter to the interests of law firms, the public, and the profession. Rather, the committee concluded, retirement, change of status, and other end-of-career issues should be matters decided by applying specific performance criteria to specific individuals on a case-by-case basis. In the committee's words:

> We do not suggest that partnership is, or should be, a guarantee of life tenure. [We are] aware of the economics of law practice and the need for senior partners to pass on client responsibilities to younger partners. Nevertheless ... a senior partner can and should be evaluated individually in accordance with his or her unique attributes and interests and the firm's generally applicable performance criteria, including the full range of strategic and tactical legal abilities and lawyering skills. Criteria such as billable hours, business generation, *pro bono*

> activities, as well as the ability to create or maintain client relationships and the willingness to involve other lawyers in them and transition them to others, administrative activities, mentoring, collegiality, recruiting activities, marketing, and other functions that support their firm's morale, reputation, growth, stability and profitability, are all relevant. These performance criteria, and not age, should help determine a professional's employment status, duties and compensation in conjunction with the needs of the particular firm.
>
> ... Whether one considers a retirement age of 65, 68, 70 or 72, it must be readily recognized that every individual partner's situation is different, as each has different attributes and provides varying utility to the ongoing well-being of the firm.

It is hard to disagree in principle with the findings and recommendation of the committee. In practice, however, implementing the committee's recommendation may be quite difficult, especially in a small firm. Most of the members of the committee are professionals who are members of or work at firms with more than 100 lawyers. When a firm gets to be of that size, there is a management structure in place. Associates and, in many cases, partners receive regular performance evaluations and face-to-face reviews. Life in a big firm is generally more sstructured and routinized, governed by formal policies and practices.

By comparison, the small firms that make up a huge majority of law practice entities in the United States (see Chapter 2) are a different sort of beast. Many of them operate on very informal terms and often have no written operating agreement, or if they do have one, the agreement is usually bare bones at best. They share profits and losses pro rata. Decisions are reached based upon consensus of the partners or are voted on by the partners. Partners are all "at risk," although that risk may be mitigated in the LLP, LLC, or PLLC forms of organization. These are all commonly recognized indicia of partnership.

Many of these small firms are organized around one or two principal "rainmakers" who control most of the business. More likely than not, lawyers within these firms practice in "silos," having little involvement with the clients of others in the firm.

I believe the committee's recommendations are well-founded and well supported. That said, small firms simply do not have the management or governance structures in place to effectively implement partner performance reviews. Status, compensation, and power in such firms are usually driven by a lawyer's ability to generate business.

When key leaders in such firms retire, it is usually accomplished by merging their firm into a larger one. If the rainmaker and his or her firm have done a proper job bringing along younger talent, the alternative practice is to transfer client contacts and ongoing matters to a younger lawyer in the firm who agrees to pay the retiring lawyer a percentage of fees generated from the older lawyer's client base.

The next chapter presents a proposal for an alternative arrangement to handle retirements in smaller firms, and possibly in some larger ones.

Chapter 10

"EMERITUS STATUS"— THE ALTERNATIVE RETIREMENT PLAN

As part of my preparation for this book, I informally surveyed retirement practices of a wide range of firms across the country. In some cases, I met personally with firm management. In other cases, my information was gathered through consulting assignments. Finally, I conducted an e-mail survey of some 100 larger firms (over 150 lawyers). In all, I documented the practices of more than sixty-five law firms.

Of the firms surveyed, one-third had no formal retirement policy or program, one-third had retirement policies that were optional (i.e., partners retired when they wanted to under a predetermined plan), and one-third had mandatory retirement policies. Most of the firms with mandatory policies allowed partners to stay on as "of counsel," if the rest of the partners approved of the arrangement. Among this group, virtually all of counsel arrangements were negotiated on an ad hoc basis. That said, virtually all of the firms with mandatory plans indicated that they were reevaluating their policies and considering alternatives.

About 15 percent of the firms surveyed described what I have come to call "emeritus status" plans. Most of these plans require partners to resign their equity status at a certain age—usually sixty-five or sixty-seven—after participating in an orderly practice transition phase, typically beginning between ages sixty and sixty-five. Having resigned from equity status, emeritus partners can continue to practice law with their firms on a reduced schedule.

As for compensation, about half the group members pay emeritus partners a salary and discretionary bonus, based upon objective and subjective factors. The rest pay their emeritus partners based upon a formula that takes into account working-lawyer collections and fees collected from clients that were originated by the partner during his or her career.

Whatever policies and practices a firm might adopt, it is wise to document a policy and memorialize it in a formal draft agreement. Emeritus plans work best when their terms are set well in advance of the time at which any individual partner might seek to alter his or her status with the firm. If a firm waits too long, there is a strong likelihood that a new policy will be viewed as an ad hoc agreement reached to handle a single individual. Once that idea gets set in partners' minds, they are likely to assume that any future arrangements will be "negotiable" based upon personal circumstances. It is far better to have a long-standing policy in place that governs all partners.

Such a formal policy should address the following issues:

- **a)** Term of the emeritus agreement
- **b)** Eligibility for emeritus status
  - **i)** Age
  - **ii)** Vesting/length of service
- **c)** Mutual mandatory notice of termination or the agreement
- **d)** Emeritus title and status, both within the firm and as presented to clients
- **e)** Guidelines and procedures for identifying successors to client relationships
- **f)** Definition of and metrics for measuring success at client transitioning
- **g)** Performance expectations vis-à-vis metrics
- **h)** Compensation of the emeritus partner
- **i)** New client originations after transition
  - **i)** As sole originator
  - **ii)** As joint originator
  - **iii)** Sunset provision of origination credits
- **j)** Business generated from clients for whom partner was originator before the transition

- **k)** Work performed, billed, and collected as working lawyer
- **l)** Required approvals
  - **i)** Client intake
  - **ii)** Matter staffing
  - **iii)** Fee arrangements
  - **iv)** Write-ups/write-downs
  - **v)** "Credit" attributions
- **m)** Transition payments
  - **i)** Capital
  - **ii)** Undistributed income
- **n)** Pay status (i.e., K-1 partner, W-2 employee, or 1099 contractor)
- **o)** Benefits continuation
  - **i)** Health insurance
  - **ii)** Disability insurance
- **p)** Continued participation in firm defined-contribution plans
- **q)** Business development and client transition allowances
- **r)** Firm administrative support
  - **i)** Office
  - **ii)** Secretary
  - **iii)** Computer/technology support
  - **iv)** Office services
- **s)** Use of firm resources
  - **i)** Authority to use associates and timekeepers
  - **ii)** Supervisory authority
- **t)** Professional liability status and commercial liability indemnification
- **u)** Accountability and reporting relationships
  - **i)** Executive Committee
  - **ii)** Management Committee
  - **iii)** Managing partner(s)
  - **iv)** Compensation Committee

v) Renewal provisions for the emeritus agreement
    i) Upon request of partner
    ii) Upon request of the firm
w) Termination provisions
    i) Upon request of partner
    ii) Upon request of the firm
x) Grievance procedure

Appendix B of this book provides a model emeritus agreement form.

Having an emeritus plan in place well in advance also provides partners who may be contemplating a change of status with a clear-cut program that they can factor into their personal financial and retirement planning. One size fits all, and everyone knows what the deal is. Nobody gets a line-item veto or a chance to change the program at the last minute.

Making the emeritus plan mandatory at a certain age may expose the plan to legal challenge. It is better to leave the decision up to the individual partner, *provided, of course, that the partner is still performing at a level one would expect of a full equity partner*. As the New York State Bar Association report points out, using age-based "triggers" is probably a discriminatory practice. If there is an issue with respect to an individual partner's performance, however, the firm is within its rights to deal with the issue through compensation adjustment or through a change of status. This presumes that the firm has adopted clear standards for performance and has fairly applied such standards to all partners.

However the decision to elect emeritus status is made, having such a policy provides an alternative status that can be attractive to both the firm and the individual partner. A partner who wants to "scale down" has a predefined program that he or she can evaluate. A firm that has a partner whose practice is on the wane has an alternative other than outright termination.

Chapter 11 INTEGRATING COMPENSATION PLANS WITH RETIREMENT POLICIES

This chapter describes various ways that law firms can fund retirement or buyout of founding partners while they are still active contributors to their firms. It will cover such techniques as paying "premium" compensation, using life insurance as a funding mechanism, a plan called a rabbi trust, and a plan that mimics a stock transfer in a closely held corporation. As with all other techniques for dealing with founders, the appropriate plan should be customized to fit the particular needs and finances of the individual firm and of its founders. There is no single best practice. I have included these techniques because I have seen them applied successfully in a number of firms.

This book is not about law firm compensation plans. That is a much larger subject. However, one cannot address the full scope of retirement and succession planning without considering how and when "retirement" compensation is paid. The quotation marks around the word "retirement" are meant to point out that compensation for past service, compensation for fronting the capital needed to start up a law firm, or compensation for creating goodwill and other intangible assets needn't be deferred until someone has ceased the practice of law or has stepped down from equity status. In many ways, it may be preferable to structure a plan whereby certain key players—most notably firm founders—are compensated for their entrepreneurial efforts while they are still practicing law and contributing to the economic well-being of their law firms.

The following are among the reasons why this approach is a good idea.

1. Waiting to fund these payments until post-retirement creates an ever-growing unfunded liability for the firm. Such a liability can impede the firm's ability to attract lateral partners or potential merger candidates.
2. Starting payments earlier provides a more certain outcome for the recipient, who usually does not want to wait for payments to be made after he or she is no longer an equity partner.
3. The generation(s) of partners most likely to benefit from the entrepreneurial efforts of the founder(s) will be the ones who bear most of the financial burden, rather than "kicking the can down the road" to future generations of partners.
4. Founders contribute to the income stream that pays them.

Needless to say, making such a distinction for founders may rankle younger partners who joined the firm after its founding, especially when there is no plan in place for them. It is far better, however, to deal with these issues while the founders are active and contributing, rather than waiting until they are facing retirement. It is also preferable to have some "pay-as-you-go" aspects to retirement planning rather than to create a huge unfunded liability.

Mechanically, prefunding the founders' benefit can be accomplished by paying premium compensation directly to the founders, i.e., compensation paid out before making current income distributions to all the partners for current efforts. Another effective way to accomplish prefunding is to use life insurance products, having the firm pay premiums on a whole-life policy covering a founder's life. Should the partner die before retirement, the proceeds of the policy are used to fund the firm's buyout obligation. Once a founder retires, he or she assumes ownership of the policy and its cash value. The only drawback with this prefunding mechanism is that policy premiums are not tax deductible when they are paid. The good news for the founder, however, is that the cash value can be withdrawn tax-free.

Yet another prefunding mechanism is the creation of a rabbi trust. In such an arrangement, the firm would contribute a certain amount each year into a deferred compensation trust on behalf of the founder. Trust assets are isolated from general creditors and are invested to yield an income stream that builds the value of the trust over time. At a certain date in the future or upon retirement of the founder, the trust is used to fund a stream of deferred compensation payments to the founder. If the founder leaves the firm prematurely, funds invested in the trust can revert to the firm. It should be carefully noted that rabbi trusts are quite complex arrangements, and any law firm considering one should definitely seek advice from tax counsel and professional investment advisers.

The foregoing notwithstanding, several firms that are just starting up have found a more direct and fair way to handle equity transfers when partners come and go. The technique is best put in place when the firm is established, but it is possible to adapt such a plan to a firm that already exists.

The plan essentially mimics stock transfers in a closely held corporation. Here's how it works:

1. When the firm is established, the founding partners create a fixed number of ownership shares, say one thousand shares, and allocate them among themselves as they wish. These ownership shares govern percentage ownership interests in the assets of the firm and can be designated voting or nonvoting shares.
2. Each founder agrees to contribute a fixed amount of cash capital, in proportion to his or her ownership shares, to finance the start-up of the firm.
3. Over the course of years, the firm may require additional capital contributions from the partners. In addition, as is true of any law firm, annual distributions to the partners generally fall below their relative shares of income earned. Any earnings left undistributed at year-end are credited to each partner's capital account, along with any additional cash capital contributions.
4. Since clients never pay for services on the day they are rendered, the firm will necessarily build up "accrual" assets, namely the value of work performed but not yet billed—unbilled work in progress (WIP)—and the value of work billed but not yet collected—fee accounts receivable (A/R). These two asset classes essentially represent a form of deferred compensation to the firm's owners, since the costs associated with creating these assets have already been borne by them over the course of the prior year(s).
5. At the end of each year, the capital accounts are aggregated, and the resulting value is divided by the number of ownership shares outstanding. This sets the cash value per share.

6. Also, at the end of each year, the values of WIP and A/R are adjusted downward to reflect the amount of fee revenue they are likely to produce. Typically, this adjustment is somewhere around 20 to 25 percent. (For the moment, we'll assume we're not dealing with any contingency-fee matters.) Adjusted WIP and A/R are aggregated, and the resulting value is divided by the number of ownership shares outstanding. This sets the accrual value per share.
7. If a new partner is admitted, he or she is assigned a number of ownership shares that are deducted pro rata from the ownership shares of the existing partners.
8. In consideration for his or her ownership shares, the new partner contributes cash in an amount equal to the cash value per share multiplied by the number of ownership shares he or she has just received. That cash is allocated among the other partners in proportion to the number of ownership shares they have ceded to the new partner.
9. Also, in consideration for his or her new ownership shares, the new partner's future compensation—as will be determined by the firm's partner compensation system—will be reduced by an amount equal to the accrual value per share multiplied by the number of ownership shares he or she has just received. This amount can be spread over a number of years. Any future compensation that is thus deferred by the new partner is then reallocated each year to the remaining partners in accordance with their relative ownership shares.
10. When a partner retires from the firm, the firm pays him or her an amount equal to the cash value per share multiplied by the number of ownership shares he or she still retains. This amounts to a tax-free return of capital.
11. In addition, the retiring partner also receives an amount equal to the accrual value per share multiplied by the number of ownership shares he or she still retains, prorated over several months or years. This second payment may be quite substantial and represents taxable compensation to the retiring partner. The good news is that these payments are already prefunded out of the WIP and A/R accumulated by the firm.

This technique has a number of distinct advantages. First, new partners purchase their ownership interests directly from the existing partners, thus reducing the end-of-the-day payout when they retire. Second, the deferred retirement compensation has already been prefunded by the accumulation of new accrual assets. Third, the value of the firm's assets is calculated each year, so each partner knows the value of his or her interest in the firm at the close of each year. Finally, the firm assets that are used to redeem shares of retiring partners have been created by those same partners over the course of their careers, or those partners have already been paid for ceding a portion of their ownership interests in prior years.

There are some other factors that may complicate matters a bit, but they can be dealt with. For example, if the firm takes a substantial number of matters on contingency, the valuation of WIP gets much more complicated. First, there's the issue of computing what the case(s) might actually produce. Then, there's the issue of allowing for the inevitable "dry wells" that inhabit contingency-fee dockets.

Another issue is affordability. As the firm grows, its accrual assets also grow in value. The important management issue for the firm is to diligently manage its billing and collection policies and practices to make sure that these assets are not growing simply because the firm has become lax in "business hygiene" habits. If accrual assets get too high, the amount of money that a new partner needs to defer in compensation may make equity partnership unaffordable.

Finally, there's the issue of intangible values. Throughout the years, a law firm's name recognition and reputation should enable it to attract and retain clients and referral sources. We are not talking about the ability of individual partners to attract business to the firm. That said, the firm's "brand" in the market could be such that it alone attracts clients to the firm. When that happens, the intangible asset of goodwill is created. The thorny issue then becomes how to value "goodwill" and how to transfer the value of goodwill from one generation of partners to another.

Whether or not it is possible to create goodwill in a law firm and the related issues surrounding its valuation have been the subjects of many court cases involving disputes among law partners and between law partners and their former spouses. These cases are far too many to cite, and although this book will never resolve the goodwill debate, it is worth mentioning as an issue that may need to be addressed. Please refer to Appendix D for references and resources that deal with goodwill in a variety of valuation contexts.

Chapter 12
SELLING YOUR LAW FIRM

I have mentioned previously that it is now permissible in a number of jurisdictions to sell a law firm. The purchaser of the firm must be a lawyer or another law firm, and ethically, the sale of the firm cannot be construed to be a sale of client relationships. This chapter is really meant to be a guide for the solo practitioner or founder of a small firm. Larger firms are usually "sold" by way of a merger with another firm—either one of equal size or a larger firm. Mergers are much more complex transactions and are outside this book's scope. That said, some of the management principles espoused in this chapter, especially those aimed at creating lasting value, should be on the menu for firms of all sizes.

The ideal time to start planning for selling a firm is when the firm is in its early and active stages of existence. Waiting until the last minute will most assuredly limit the number of options available. Furthermore, with a possible sale on the long-term horizon, the founders may choose different strategic planning and management initiatives than they might otherwise choose, if the goal is to operate the firm to maximize current incomes of the partners.

To effectively sell a law firm, the firm's owners and managers need to be thinking about creating long-term sustainable value, and not just paying out the maximum amount of income each year. Investments need to be made in establishing a market identity for the firm that has value separate and apart from the owners (see the discussion of "goodwill" in Chapter 11). These investments may include:

1. marketing initiatives aimed at establishing a "brand" identity for the firm in its area(s) of specialty;

2. cultivating and maintaining a network of referral sources;
3. joining and becoming active in one of the national or international networks of law and/or accounting firms, such as MSI Global, Primerus, et. al.;
4. investing in training and career development of younger lawyers who will be valuable contributors to the practice of the acquiring firm;
5. creating proprietary systems, procedures, and technologies that uniquely support the practice of the firm, like such as document drafting systems, form books, systems to manage cases in the pipeline, etc; and
6. investing in and focus on creating institutional approaches for managing for the long term, especially in the key areas of client development, talent development, and work-flow management.

These are but a few examples of how a firm can invest in creating lasting value that a buyer might be interested in acquiring. Needless to say, these and other techniques require the diversion of otherwise distributable profits into investments that will benefit the firm over the long haul.

Another important step is to have in place a fully formed law practice entity, like a PLLC, LLC, LLP, or PC. Even a solo practitioner should have a formal operating agreement that contemplates bringing in new co-owners and affords a well-planned exit strategy (see *Model Partnership Agreements for New York Law Firms* [Giuliani 2008]).

A solo practitioner should already have a plan in place that takes care of the firm's clients if something happens to the solo practitioner. This is like having an estate plan and executor agreement for the law firm, and it simply makes ethical sense to have such a plan in place.

The sale of a law practice is generally part of an orderly plan for the founder's (or founders') retirement. First, the founder or the owners of the practice must decide what is meant by "retirement" and then structure a sale transaction that aids in accomplishing this goal. Does the founder expect to completely cease the practice of law? Is emeritus or of counsel status a goal? Or does the founder simply want to cash out and continue to practice on a reduced schedule?

Next, the founder should develop an exit strategy that accomplishes the goal. This can involve transferring equity to a junior partner or an associate already at the firm. Alternatively, it may involve a search for a merger partner or an outside lawyer to acquire the practice. In the extreme, it may involve a detailed and orderly plan to gradually dissolve the firm and refer clients to lawyers in other firms.

In any of these strategies, the founder will have to identify a successor, if one is not already obvious. If the firm already has a junior partner, the choice may be clear. That said, if the junior partner cannot afford the terms of sale, the founder will need to look outside for a buyer. That would require the firm to conduct an orderly search for a successor.

The process of finding a successor is similar to a strategic expansion process involving acquisition of lateral practitioners with portable practices. The firm first needs to formulate a search plan. Such a plan would involve answering the following questions:

1. What do you want to accomplish and why? What are your retirement and succession goals, and how do you plan to achieve them?
2. What alternatives make sense initially? Merger? Outright sale to another lawyer or law firm? Passing the torch to a junior partner? Winding down?
3. What is the ideal profile of the person or firm to take over the practice? Age? Experience? Practice specialty?
4. What does the firm have to offer that person or practice? Referral network? Will vault? Proprietary systems or software?
5. In twenty-five words or less, what is the seller's "pitch" to the successor? Essentially, this is a statement of all of the above, coupled with a statement as to how the seller envisions the successor helping to accomplish the goals. It should also state why the seller has selected the successor, as opposed to other possibilities.

The purpose of having a search plan is to make sure that the selling firm has a convincing story to tell prospective buyers, even though those prospects may be well known to the seller. It also establishes a mutuality of interest between both parties and makes the seller's goals and personal plans clear. This may sound like an overly formal way to go about selling a law practice, but the seller needs to think through what he or she wants to accomplish and articulate that objective so that the prospective buyer(s) will see the value of what is offered.

The next step in the process is to establish what a reasonable, qualified, and informed person might pay to acquire the practice. Chapter 5 of this book covers the basics of the valuation of a law practice. The seller(s) might want to engage an accountant or other professional to prepare an independent valuation of the practice. That should add credibility to the seller's asking price, and the valuation methodology should provide various detail points of negotiation for both parties. In the end, there are three major terms on which the two parties need to agree: the valuation (i.e., purchase price), the plan for transfer of ownership, and the method of financing the transaction.

The purchase price is usually determined in a valuation exercise, similar to what was covered in Chapter 5. As for the transfer of ownership, there are generally two basic options, depending upon whether the firm in question is an incorporated entity or a partnership or sole proprietorship.

In its simplest form, buying an incorporated law practice can be structured as a straightforward cash transaction, much like buying any other business. The buyer and seller agree upon a price for the shares in the corporation. In consideration for cash, stock, or other valuable assets, the seller transfers title of the business to the buyer.

The buyer records the new asset on a balance sheet, along with any debt incurred to finance the purchase. The seller realizes a capital gain on the sale of his or her stock and pays tax on that capital gain. The tricky question is how to determine the tax basis of the shares sold, so that the capital gain can be measured. This is a task best left up to professional accountants.

The purchases and sales of unincorporated practices are more complex transactions. Many law firms are organized as PLLCs or LLPs, which are "pass-through" entities for tax purposes (i.e., owners pay income tax on the firm's earnings at the personal level, and there is no tax assessed at the entity level). Also, such entities typically do not issue shares of stock to their owners, which they then can sell to others at a price that will realize either a capital gain or a capital loss.

In the sale of a law firm organized as a PLLC, LLP, or LLC, the seller first transfers his or her interest in hard assets (e.g., cash, client costs advanced, furniture and fixtures, equipment, etc.), generally at a loss. The carrying value of these assets on the selling firm's balance sheet does not reflect current market value. Rather, it reflects the historical cost of the items, reduced for accumulated depreciation. In addition, there may be unamortized costs of leasehold improvements that will expire when the seller gives up the office lease. Thus, in all likelihood, the purchase price paid for hard assets will be different from the values carried on the seller's books, affording the seller a capital gain or loss on the sale of the assets, not the entire firm.

In this case, the seller also transfers his or her interest in unbilled and uncollected fees, which will eventually turn into taxable income for the buyer. Because these taxes will have to be paid, the buyer is not likely to pay cash or other after-tax assets to acquire these pretax assets. That said, these assets are likely to be worth considerable sums of money, when they are eventually collected. The challenge is in how to pay the seller.

Perhaps the most straightforward arrangement is to agree that, as the unbilled work in progress and accounts receivable are collected, the majority of the fees thus collected—less an allowance for work done by the buyer after the transaction date—will be paid to the seller. This effectively transfers the risk of collection, and a lot of the value, to the seller. Unfortunately, this arrangement forces the buyer to come up with working capital to finance the operation of the new firm, money he or she may not have.

Because of the tax and financing issues involved with selling the work in progress and accounts receivable, this part of the transaction is most commonly handled through a deferred compensation arrangement. Typically, the seller agrees to continue working for the buyer as of counsel for two years or so at a sufficient level of compensation. This allows the seller to recover the value of unbilled and uncollected accounts, plus any payments for "goodwill." The deferred compensation payments are taxable earnings to the seller and deductible expenses to the buyer. This type of payment plan is often referred to as an "earn-out" plan, as opposed to a buyout plan.

Previous chapters have discussed ways in which a partner or group of partners transfers ownership to incoming partners by having the firm pay bonus compensation to the older generation for a period of time, usually three to five years. This "earn-out" plan is simply a variant on that kind of ownership transfer. In addition, rather than buy individual after-tax assets outright, the buyer can work out a deferred payment plan to return the seller's accumulated capital account over the same period.

Under an "earn-out" plan, the seller may be required to continue to work on some matters during the period of deferred compensation. When that is the case, the buyer also has to negotiate how the seller will be paid for these services. The more common arrangements call for a flat salary that covers the "earn-out," plus a bonus equivalent to about two-thirds of what the continuing firm collects on the billable time logged by the seller. Occasionally, the seller is also paid a "commission" of about 10 percent on fees collected from any new clients he or she originates for the buyer after the transaction date.

The "earn-out" plans are generally preferred by the buyer, because they spread the financing of the purchase over a reasonably long period of time. Sellers often like this kind of arrangement, too, because it avoids having to pay income taxes on a large lump-sum payment. They also get to decide just how hard they want to work after ceding control of their firms. Some like to remain active. Others would prefer to sail into the sunset and clip the coupons of their deferred compensation plan. The bottom line is that both sides are able to comfortably achieve their mutual objectives.

The only significant risk is of the buyer so mismanaging the firm that he or she is unable to make the "earn-out" payments to the seller. For that reason, these plans typically have a provision that gives the seller the power to either rescind the sale or force a dissolution of the firm if the buyer fails to keep his or her side of the bargain. This way, the seller gets to capture whatever value remains after ousting the mismanaging buyer.

Here are some words of advice for those who are contemplating selling their practices:

1. Do not attempt to sell your practice without retaining competent transactional and tax counsel. Accountants can be helpful in valuing your firm and advising on tax issues. Elder-law lawyers are good advisers in the area of estate and post-retirement financial planning. Finally, you may need a lawyer well versed in local corporate and/or partnership law to advise on terms and maybe "paper the deal."
2. Do not represent yourself. There is truth in the adage that a lawyer who represents himself has a fool for a client. You are too close to your practice to be objective in negotiating terms. This is the only time in your life that you will sell your practice. There are others out there—accountants, lawyers, and other advisers—who have experience in selling businesses. Let them guide and advise you.
3. Put everything in writing, even among family members. Memories are often short, sometimes conveniently so. Buyers can also suffer from "selective recall" when they are forced to make "earn-out" payments when business isn't so good. There is no substitute for having a written agreement, especially when things don't turn out the way you expected.

4. Make sure you are able to regain ownership of the practice if your buyer defaults, commits malpractice, etc. In any kind of "earn-out" plan, you, the seller, are at risk throughout the "earn-out" period. Bad things can happen, and you will need a preplanned remedy in case the seller fails to live up to the bargain.
5. If you bring in a partner, have a plan to *gradually* cede voting control over time—say, three years. Since you are not getting paid for all of your equity in a lump sum, you will need to retain control of your practice for some period of time until the seller has effectively purchased most of your equity interest. This goes hand in glove with the provision that lets you regain the practice if the buyer fails.
6. Do your due diligence; know your buyer well. If you are counting on the sale of your practice to provide retirement income, you need to be reasonably certain that the buyer has the skills to manage your practice successfully and that he or she has the financial wherewithal to pay you, even though the continuing practice may suffer some loss of business. Finally, you need to be sure of the character and ethics of the person to whom you are selling your life's work. Forewarned is forearmed.

Chapter 13

SPECIAL CONSIDERATIONS FOR CONTINGENCY-FEE PRACTICES

The existence of contingency-fee arrangements in a law firm complicates firm valuation and succession planning. As with any type of professional service, the costs of providing the service (i.e., salaries, rent, other operating costs, etc.) have already been paid by the firm long before the resulting fee is collected. In an hourly based or flat-fee-based practice, the likelihood that the fee will ultimately be collected is fairly high. In a contingency-fee practice, however, the prospect of collecting the fee is much less certain.

When a partner leaves a firm, he or she has historically invested in creating fees that will bear fruit after he or she leaves, and previous chapters have suggested how departing partners can be compensated for their historical investment in creating billable work. The tricky thing with contingency practices—especially those residing in law practices that have a mix of hourly, flat-fee, and contingency work—is that the value of contingency cases cannot reasonably be determined as of the date of retirement.

There are two basic challenges:

1. The collection of the fee is not assured.
2. The historical cost of providing the service, as measured by the value of time and costs invested in the case(s), may have no relation to the fee ultimately collected.

So what mechanism can be applied to make economic sense of contingency fees that are collected after someone retires? How do you bring in a new partner when the firm's practice is all contingency based, without actually placing a value on the case docket?

Here is how one straight-contingency firm handled it:

Drake & Gander, LLP

A CASE STUDY INVOLVING PURE CONTINGENCY PRACTICE

Paul Drake and Louise Gander have been in a law partnership for ten years. They concentrate on representing plaintiffs who have been injured or killed due to negligence, defective products, misleading labeling, etc. They started out representing individual plaintiffs, but after a favorable result in a case involving four people injured when a structure collapsed at a resort hotel, they started receiving referrals of many more cases involving multiple plaintiffs.

In a slow year, Paul and Louise equally divide about $2 million in profits. In many years, however, they earn as much as $5 million. Considering the firm's case docket, Paul and Louise could possibly split $7 million in profits in the current year or the next, if one very large case gets resolved. They estimate that, conservatively, the current case docket could eventually produce $15 million in fees over the next three years, even if they don't accept any new cases.

All case costs advanced are self-funded by the two partners, and the firm typically carries about $500,000 on its balance sheet in case-cost accounts receivable. The firm has no debt and has been able to distribute all of its earned income to the two partners within two months of the end of each year. As a cushion, the two partners leave $300,000 in operating capital in the firm to fund day-to-day operations and allow for $10,000 monthly draws to each partner.

As cases are settled, Paul and Louise reimburse the firm for any case costs and immediately distribute 80 percent of the fee recovery to themselves, leaving the remaining 20 percent in the firm to finance operations. About the time that quarterly estimated income tax payments are due (i.e., April 15, June 15, September 15), they consider the amount of cash on hand and decide on how much to pay themselves in a special distribution to cover estimated taxes. The year-end distribution is generally sufficient to cover the January 15 estimated payment and still pay out 80 percent of the firm's net income for the year.

Vera Jones and Adam Smith have been associates with the firm for five years, and Paul and Louise would like to offer them an equity stake in the firm. Both associates make base salaries of $200,000, plus discretionary bonuses for their work on successful cases. Including bonuses, health insurance and other benefits, they both make around $300,000 per year.

The firm's accountant has prepared a pro forma balance sheet that estimates what the net assets of the firm will be at the close of the current year, when Vera and Adam will become partners. That pro forma balance sheet shows the following:

Cash	$ 1,400,000
Client costs advanced	500,000
Furniture, fixtures, and equipment (net)	300,000
Total Assets	2,200,000
Undistributed net income	(800,000)
Retirement plan payable	(200,000)
Total Liabilities	(1,000,000)
Net Assets	1,200,000

The problem, in the case of Drake & Gander, is one of affordability. How can Paul and Louise sell off enough of a percentage of the firm to allow Vera and Adam to maintain reasonable compensation and still afford to purchase their equity?

After consultation with their accountant, Paul and Louise drafted the following terms of admission:

1. As of January 1 of the following year, Vera and Adam would be offered the opportunity to each acquire a 15 percent interest in the firm, with Paul and Louise retaining 70 percent ownership and voting control of the firm.
2. Vera and Adam will each be entitled to a 15 percent share of future profits of the firm, which would mean that, even in a slow year, they would each receive $300,000 (15 percent of $2 million profit).
3. In consideration for their 15 percent equity shares, Vera and Adam agree to each forgo $180,000 (15 percent of net assets) in otherwise payable compensation over the next five years. Thus, each might pay taxes on $300,000 a year in compensation, but only receive $264,000 in cash. Of course, they could receive much more in compensation if enough cases are resolved favorably.

This arrangement solves the issue of affordability, but what about fairness? Paul and Louise are sitting on a case docket that could produce $15 million in fees in a relatively short time. Vera and Adam, other than working on these cases, have taken no risk and have had no hand in financing the firm while these cases were active. Should Paul and Louise simply give them a 30 percent interest in the case docket? Can Vera and Adam afford to buy their interests in the case docket? The answer to both questions is no.

Paul and Louise's solution is as follows:

1. Paul and Louise will contribute the smaller cases in the docket—those that they expect to resolve within the next year. These cases are expected to result in fees of $4 million, which would be allocated to the new partnership to cover operating expenses

and profit of about $2 million. Note that $600,000 in operating expenses (associate salaries and benefits) has been eliminated by admitting Vera and Paul.

2. The remaining cases will be carved out of the docket, and fees collected from these cases will be shared as follows:
   a. If the case resolves within the first year of the new partnership, 12.5 percent of the fee will be allocated to the new partnership and 87.5 percent will be shared equally between Paul and Louise.
   b. If the case resolves within the second year of the new partnership, 25 percent of the fee will be allocated to the new partnership and 75 percent will be shared equally between Paul and Louise.
   c. If the case resolves within the third year of the new partnership, 50 percent of the fee will be allocated to the new partnership and 50 percent will be shared equally between Paul and Louise.
   d. After the third year of the new partnership, all fees will be allocated to the new partnership.

This arrangement accomplishes two things. First, it enables Paul and Louise to retain the lion's share of the fees resulting from a case docket that they have invested in. Second, it provides some compensation to the new partnership for work done on the carved out cases to resolve them.

Finally, there is the question as to what happens if either Paul or Louise decides to retire. Should a retired partner continue to participate in fees received after he or she ceases work?

Paul and Louise resolved this issue by agreeing to sell their partnership interests back to the firm gradually over a three-year period after they retire. The percentage interests will be acquired in part by paying cash for the retired partner's share of net assets as of the date of retirement. The remaining consideration will be a continuing—albeit declining—share in the profits of the firm, as the partner's ownership interest is redeemed.

In the first three years of a partner's retirement, the continuing firm will acquire 25 percent of the retired partner's interest, and his or her share of profits will decline by 25 percent in each year. In January of the fourth year of retirement, the firm will acquire the final 25 percent of the partner's interest, and he or she will no longer share in profits.

This case study demonstrates how one pure contingency firm handled the admission and retirement issues associated with transferring ownership between two generations of partners. The firm dealt with the issue of affordability and the issue of how to compensate founders for their investment in a very profitable case docket. Future success will depend upon how able the new generation is at picking and resolving good cases.

The issue of contingency cases gets quite complicated, however, when one is dealing with a law firm that has a blend of hourly work and contingency work. In a "blended" firm, the fees collected from hourly work provide a base of "normal" operations that pays the bills and provides a level of base compensation, while the lawyers who work on contingency matters handle cases that the firm has decided present a favorable risk/reward balance.

At this point we need to have a more extensive digression into the economics of contingency fees. Time for another case study.

Butcher, Baker & Chandler

A CASE STUDY ON CONTINGENCY FEES IN A "MIXED" PRACTICE

Butcher, Baker & Chandler is a fifty-lawyer firm with seventeen equity partners. The firm has a substantial corporate finance and transactional practice, as well as a litigation department, which handles big-ticket commercial and securities litigation. About eight years ago, Newton Baker, the firm's principal trial lawyer, successfully defended a groundbreaking, high visibility intellectual property infringement suit in the computer software licensing area, thereby establishing the firm as a major player in that area. As a result, there has been a steady stream of contacts and case referrals with huge sums of money at stake.

In 2002, the firm agreed for the first time to take a case on contingency—a technology licensing dispute in which the plaintiff was seeking $20 million in back royalties and prejudgment interest. The fee arrangement was a straight one-third contingent fee, which would cover all services and costs advanced. Since that time, the firm has accepted four additional contingency-fee matters on similar terms, all involving substantial claims. None of the cases were deemed to be "easy wins" when they were accepted.

In 2007, Baker and his team of one additional partner, Melanie Hamilton, two associates, and two paralegals won an $18 million jury award in the first case, resulting in a $6 million contingency fee for the firm, which was collected in 2008. Over the life of the case, the firm expended the following resources:

Firm Expenditures Related to a Personal Injury Case

Year	Time Value	Costs Advanced	Total Investment
2002	$ 55,000	$ 2,000	$ 57,000
2003	765,000	90,000	855,000
2004	815,000	120,000	935,000
2005	900,000	95,000	995,000
2006	250,000	10,000	260,000
2007	20,000	5,000	25,000
Total	$ 2,805,000	$ 322,000	$ 3,127,000

Over the course of the case, all client costs advanced were financed by the firm. Costs advanced in conjunction with the other four cases presently total $625,000 and are likely to amount to more than $1 million before the cases are resolved.

Each year, the firm develops a profit plan and, based upon financial forecasts, computes a standard hourly rate schedule. In computing the rate schedule, the firm takes into account direct compensation and benefits, an allocation of overhead and infrastructure costs, and a target profit margin of 35 percent. The hourly rates computed during the planning process are viewed as guideline rates. Each partner may adjust actual billing upward or downward, within certain limits, from the guideline value of time spent on a matter. On average, the firm realizes 95 percent of its guideline rates.

Newton Baker has come to the partnership and asked that the $6 million fee be allocated outside of the firm's normal profit allocation system and that substantial bonuses be paid to those who served on the trial team. The partnership met and agreed that there should be special bonus compensation paid to those who served on the trial team. The firm agreed on the amounts to be paid to the associates and paralegals. They could not agree, however, on a rationale for determining a fair allocation of the fee among the partners. Newton Baker's profit-sharing percentage is 8 percent and Melanie Hamilton's percentage is 4 percent.

What is fair? How much "bonus" money is really available?

The partnership has already recognized that the trial team members have earned a special bonus because of the result achieved from their extraordinary efforts, unique expertise, and creativity. Since the question of merit is not in dispute, we should begin by addressing the issue of what constitutes fair compensation for the firm. One must bear in mind that the partners who worked on the case will receive compensation in two ways, once through the normal distribution of profits and again through a special bonus distribution. Thus, they will share in whatever sums are allocated by the firm.

One also needs to bear in mind that all the other partners footed their share of the costs to support this effort and should receive compensation for their role.

Recovery of resources invested. Few, if any, would dispute the proposition that the firm should be paid for the value of time invested in the case and reimbursed for the costs advanced. Furthermore, there should be little debate over the proper valuation of costs advanced. Where there may be some question, however, is in the proper valuation of time expended on the case.

In this matter, there are three distinct possibilities:

1. Value time charges at 65 percent of standard, so that the firm is reimbursed for direct cost and overhead only.
2. Value time charges at 95 percent of standard to reflect the firm's normal realization experience.

3. Value time charges at 100 percent of standard rates, providing the firm with a guideline profit on the invested time.

The first alternative ignores the "opportunity cost" of assigning resources to the contingency matter. Presumably, the lawyers who worked on the matter would have been productively occupied on other matters, if the firm had not accepted the contingency-fee matter. The difference between full rates and straight cost rates reflects the normal profit margin that the firm would have earned by assigning the lawyers to other cases. "Normal profit" in this instance becomes the measure of opportunity cost.

The fact that the firm normally recovers 95 percent of guideline rates on average may or may not be relevant. The goal should be to afford the firm a "normal profit" for the commitment of resources. The relevant question is, "What profit would the same lawyers have generated if they had worked on the case (or cases) that represents the next best use of their time?" If the firm is accustomed to realizing 110 percent of standard rates on hourly cases in this area, then the appropriate value for the time would be at guideline rates plus 10 percent. If other similar cases realized only 85 percent, then a 15 percent discount would be appropriate. Lacking additional information, it is best to value the time at full guideline rates.

Time value of money. In considering a proper allocation of values, it is important to recognize that the capital of the firm supported the case for nearly six years. Costs were advanced, salaries were paid, infrastructure was funded, and partners deferred compensation to support the case. Like the lawyers assigned to the case, the money invested in the case has an alternative use, whether in the form of direct outlays or deferred compensation. The firm should be compensated for the estimated income the capital could have earned if it had been invested elsewhere. The tricky issue is to determine the rate of return that would fairly compensate the firm for supplying the capital.

One way of compensating for the use of capital is to apply a rate that reflects the firm's cost of borrowing. This method presumes that the firm would have borrowed to finance the case if it lacked the capital to carry it. Furthermore, the fact set indicates that the firm financed the case with firm capital and deferred compensation. Applying a cost-of-borrowing analysis is merely one way of computing a rough estimate of the cost of financing the case.

An alternate method is to estimate the return that could have been earned, had equivalent funds been invested in some other similarly risky vehicle. This analysis presumes that one can easily measure comparative risk between two alternative investments. It also presumes that one can find alternate investment choices that have the same risk profile as a contingency-fee case. The easy way out of this dilemma is to reimburse the firm for the use of capital at a presumably risk-free rate of return (e.g., one-year yield of U.S. government securities) and make an allowance for risk separate from the allowance for capital cost (see below).

Assuming that the proper rate of return is determined to be 2.5 percent per annum (estimated moving average one-year T-bill rate from 2002 through 2007), the capital cost reimbursement portion associated with the firm's investment in the matter amounts to $308,815. This reflects what the firm would have earned had it invested its money in one-year T-bills instead of the case.

Risk premium. At this point in the analysis, there remains $2,564,185 of the fee to be allocated (the original $6 million, less the investment of $3,127,000 and capital costs of $308,815). The firm has been reimbursed for its investment, which allows for a normal profit and the carrying cost of the case based upon a risk-free rate.

When it accepted the contingency-fee matter, the firm assumed a risk that all of the partners shared. If the trial team had lost the case, all partners would have shared in the loss. Fortunately, Baker's team won. Nevertheless, the firm should receive some compensation, over and above the recovery of its investment and capital costs, for taking the risk in the first place. How do we apportion the remaining risk premium?

There are many ways in which this allocation could be settled. A simple solution would be to share the remaining premium of $2,564,185 equally between the firm and the trial team, or according to some other negotiated proportion. While this approach may be criticized as being arbitrary and unscientific, negotiated settlements are often preferable because everyone ends up feeling equally dissatisfied with the result.

A more interesting possibility would be to model the risk/reward allocation based upon an alternative-investment analysis. The idea is to determine what the firm should have expected to earn if it had invested in a comparably risky investment vehicle, instead of investing in the case. The "market return" is intended to compensate the firm for risk. Any premium over the "market return" is presumed to have been earned by the trial team.

All investors take risks. The most sophisticated of them decide in advance what kind of rate of return they need to earn on their money if they are going to beat the return they could have earned on their next best alternative investment. For example, corporate bond traders might set their required minimum return on what AAA corporate bonds are yielding and add a premium to that rate for any bonds rated less than AAA.

Stock traders, on the other hand, use a price-earnings multiple to accomplish the same thing. For example, if a common stock trades at five times earnings, the investor expects to receive a return better than 20 percent. Commercial real estate investors, by comparison, typically expect returns of about 25 percent on average. Expected yields on junk bonds are roughly in the same range.

So one might ask, "Is the risk involved with taking on this lawsuit greater or less than the risk involved with investing in commercial real estate (e.g., through a REIT investment)?" While there is room for argument, I believe that a minimum 15 percent risk premium is a reasonable expectation when dealing with contingency-fee matters, especially if the firm has other matters in the pipeline that may or may not pay off.

If we apply the 15 percent risk return, the available premium is further reduced by $2,245,746, leaving $318,438 of premium to allocate.

Summary and Pro Forma Allocation

Note that this analysis is focused on a single fee result from a single matter. In practice, one would have to consider other relevant factors, such as the following:

- What has been the firm's historical experience with contingency matters handled by the trial team? In the case study, the case result is the first in a possible series of five cases. If there had been an established track record of wins and losses, it would have to be taken into account. For example, if this case had followed a major loss, it is doubtful whether any special allocation would have been warranted.
- What is the likelihood that the trial team will prevail in other cases in which it is involved? The case study facts assume that there are already four other cases in inventory and that there may be as much as $1 million in costs advanced. Should the firm set aside a reserve to cover future losses? Can such a reserve be sheltered from current taxation?
- What are the realistic expectations of the trial lawyers involved with the cases? The more successful they become, the more mobile they become. If there is a continuing string of successes, the firm will be well-advised to allocate more to the trial team than might be suggested by the case analysis.
- What happens if a lawyer leaves the firm and takes the case with him or her? How does the firm assert its rights to fee recovery against a successor firm without creating an ethical problem with the client?
- What would have happened if one of the partners not on the trial team had retired from the firm prior to the case being resolved? How is he or she to be compensated for his or her investment in the case?

The table below summarizes how one might apportion the hypothetical fee collected in the case study, if one accepted the "market-risk" approach to isolating the risk premium.

Fee Apportionment in a Market-Risk Approach

	Total	15 Partners	Baker	Hamilton
Costs Advanced	$ 322,000	$ 283,360	$ 25,760	$ 12,880
Time Value at Cost	1,823,250	1,604,460	145,860	72,930
Cost Recovered	2,145,250	1,887,820	171,620	85,810
"Normal Profit"	981,750	863,940	78,540	39,270
Capital Cost	308,815	271,757	24,705	12,353
Risk Premium	2,245,746	1,976,257	179,660	89,830
Skill Premium	318,438	0	212,292	106,146
Case Profit	3,854,750	3,111,954	495,197	247,599
Total	$ 6,000,000	$ 4,999,774	$ 666,817	$ 333,409
Apportionment of Case Profit	100.00%	80.73%	12.85%	6.42%
Case Profit per Partner	$ 226,750	$ 207,464	$ 495,197	$ 247,599

Needless to say, this will be a very good year for Butcher, Baker & Chandler. The case result will have produced a windfall for everyone. More than $3 million of costs incurred in prior years has been recovered, and an extraordinary profit has been earned. On average, the fifteen partners who did not participate in the case will collect over $200,000 each in bonus compensation. Newton Baker and Melanie Hamilton will both receive bonuses, albeit probably less than they might have expected.

There is a bit of a dilemma as to what to do with the cost recovery, however. Bear in mind that the firm will have collected $2,145,250 in cost recovery during a year in which total costs advanced on the case only amounted to $50,000. Some firms might be tempted to distribute the entire cost recovery to the partners as additional compensation. A more prudent firm would look for ways to set aside a portion of the cost recovery to finance the other contingency cases or otherwise build firm capital to ease the burden of possible future case losses.

Of course, there are many other concerns to address in real life when it comes to financing contingency matters and sharing the rewards. This case study is an attempt to isolate the three major factors—investment recovery, capital costs, and compensation for risk—that should determine how firms share contingency fees. The case study has asked the reader to make a number of assumptions, some of which may or may not be valid in a practical setting. Also, others may view the level of and sharing of risk differently. Each situation is unique and should be analyzed in accordance with the facts at hand. One hopes, however, that the principles embodied in this case study prove useful in structuring practical solutions to this problem.

Contingency-fee practices can also pose issues when new partners are admitted to the firm. Existing partners will have accumulated sizable investments in case costs and time. A new equity partner, who may eventually share in the fees collected from existing cases without having made the initial investment, probably does not have the personal capital to contribute to effectively "buy" his or her share of the cases. Thus, as a practical matter, there needs to be economic transitional planning at both ends of the partner entry/retirement continuum.

The most common solution employed by both mixed and strictly contingency firms is to apportion case fees before and after the transition event, based upon how long the case was open during each period. For example, if a case lasts four years and a new partner is admitted at the end of the first year of the case, he or she will share in three-quarters of the resulting fee, while other partners will share in the remainder. Similarly, when a partner retires while a case is active, his or her share of the resulting fee is apportioned according to how long the case was active during his or her tenure as an equity partner.

This most common practice works best when there are a number of lower-value cases, as in an automotive personal injury practice, for example. Once one starts to consider how to deal with bigger cases, as in mass-tort, multiple-plaintiff cases, the job gets tougher. These cases often involve hundreds of thousands of dollars in advanced costs and millions of dollars in time value. Furthermore, they can last for many years, often a decade or more, so that partner comings and goings are greater in number and pose considerable complexities. It gets even more complicated if the firm is sloppy at keeping time records on contingency-fee matters.

In the event of partner admission, often certain big cases are inventoried and their resulting fees are carved out of future profits to be shared primarily by legacy partners, irrespective of how much work is done on the cases after the new partner is admitted. This poses a cash-flow burden on the incoming partner, because he or she may not be sharing significantly in profits until the legacy cases work their way through the firm.

In summary, when one is in the process of designing a partner admission or retirement plan, one needs to consider contingency-fee practice separately from other practices. Depending upon a whole range of unique circumstances, it may or may not be possible to design a workable transition plan that makes perfect economic sense. Experience shows that most solutions in this area are a result of compromise among the parties—the incoming partner(s), the legacy partner(s), and the retiring partner(s). The economic principles covered in this chapter, however, can provide a useful framework as to how to handle these situations.

Chapter 14

FINAL THOUGHTS

As stated in the Introduction of this book, I set out to identify key economic issues typically encountered by law firms when they consider how partners end their careers, as they inevitably must, and to illustrate those issues and their resolutions through several case studies. The book also touches upon economic considerations regarding transitioning new partners into law firms. The reason for including a limited treatment of partnership admission is because that is the way many small-firm and solo practitioners end up transitioning their practices.

By design, I focused mostly on economic issues, rather than the equally important issues of client succession, ethical considerations, responsibilities of solo practitioners, etc. This book also does not address legal issues that might be associated with disputes over the rights of individual partners vis-à-vis their firms. Again, these topics are much larger than the scope of this book and probably deserve their own book.

Similar to any good consulting report, however, this subject closes with a series of recommendations.

Be Sure Your Firm Has a Current Partnership Agreement or Operating Agreement.

Many small law firms still operate with "handshake" agreements or no formal agreements at all. The New York State Bar Association's book, *Model Partnership Agreements for New York Law Firms* (Giuliani 2008), makes a persuasive case for having an effective agreement in place designed to protect the law firm as an ongoing entity. It also provides a model form that can be used as a starting point for drafting such an agreement.

Having an effective agreement in place is not merely a matter of formality. It is a matter of strategic importance that ensures that the law firm can and will exist beyond the tenures of those who currently occupy it. Furthermore, it enables the law firm to pursue other strategic initiatives, like growth, market development, mergers, ancillary businesses, etc., in a manner that protects the firm's interests and those of its owners.

Law firms make up literally thousands of the small businesses that support and fuel our economy. They employ lawyers, paralegals, and support staff. They acquire assets through purchase and lease transactions. They create and use capital. Like other small businesses, they should also create wealth for their owners. By not having an effective and comprehensive operating agreement in place, law practitioners endanger their ability to create, grow, protect, and transfer the wealth that rightly emanates from their economic activity.

Be Sure Your Partnership Agreement or Operating Agreement Comprehensively Addresses What Happens When a Partner or Member Decides to Retire.

For many small law firms that have operating agreements in place, the agreements are either silent or inadequate with respect to what happens when key partners retire. Such agreements may address the rights of partners who withdraw from the firm, for whatever reason, but, in most cases, they do not comprehensively deal with what happens to the economic interests of the withdrawing partner and the continuing economic interests of the surviving entity.

In the life of a law firm, there are three major events that have significant economic consequences. They are:

- the organizing and founding of the firm itself, even though the firm may have only a single owner (i.e., solo practitioner);
- the admission of its first owner (i.e., equity partner) who was not one of the founders of the firm; and
- the retirement of one or more of the founding generation of partners.

The first of these is the seminal event that calls the firm into being and starts the process by which wealth is created. The second begins the process of transferring some of the accumulated wealth to other owners, a process that continues until the third event triggers the ultimate transfer of wealth from the original owners to a new generation. Without the second and third events, there is no viable continuing business entity. It effectively dies with its creator(s).

In many ways, the retirement of a partner is merely a reversal of the process by which that partner was admitted to the firm (i.e., acquired his or her ownership interest) in the first place. In the case of a founding partner, his or her ownership interest was created ex nihilo, rather than by economic exchange. If the firm has been successful, founders and subsequent owners have, along the way, created wealth in the form of the firm entity. It is an asset, *and it has value* that should be considered whenever new owners arrive on the scene or former owners surrender their ownership interests in the enterprise.

So, while an operating agreement may nominally address withdrawal or retirement, it does so *inadequately* if it does not recognize the process by which wealth has been created and transferred along the way.

If You are a Solo Practitioner, Make Sure You Have a Documented Plan Covering What to do with Your Practice if Something Happens to You.

Solos have a unique and extra ethical duty that practitioners in multiple-lawyer firms do not have—they need to have a clear plan in place that takes care of their clients in the event they are incapacitated or otherwise cannot continue to represent them. It is also a good idea to have such a plan in place to cover what will eventually happen once the practitioner retires.

Few trusts and estates lawyers would advise their clients to forgo a will and estate plan. Why, then, would a solo practitioner consider forgoing an "estate plan" for his or her practice? As every estate names an executor, every solo practitioner should have identified and reached an agreement with another lawyer or law firm to take over in the event of death, incapacity, or other terminating event. This agreement should be in writing and contain all information necessary for the successor lawyer(s) to step in and see that client interests are protected.

At a minimum, the practitioner should maintain and annually update the following inventory of items:

- designation of another lawyer or law firm to serve as conservator of the practice and take responsibility for winding up the practice;
- instructions as to the location and content of all key business records and client files;

- a current list of all firm assets and liabilities, checking accounts, trust accounts, escrow and deposit accounts, etc., including the host institution for each account and the account numbers
- a current list of all firm clients, including a list of active matters and the location of case/matter files
- names and addresses of all contract, part-time, and permanent employees of the practice
- name and official notice address of the landlord
- a draft release letter to be sent to all clients, notifying them of the termination of the practice and giving instructions as to how to make their preference regarding a successor lawyer known
- any other detailed instructions that may be necessary to effect a smooth transition

If a Firm Has Multiple Partners, Start Talking with Them About Personal Retirement Plans as Early as Age Fifty-Five.

Many lawyers don't want to talk about their own retirement plans. Maybe it's because they feel they have neglected their own estate and retirement planning. Maybe it's because they haven't saved enough to provide for a decent retirement. Whatever the reason for the reluctance, it is important to the preservation of the law firm that firm leaders communicate with all partners about how long they want to practice, when they expect to start scaling back, what their expectations are regarding pre- and post-retirement compensation, the existence or lack of personal financial plans, etc.

Investment counselors will generally agree that the wise person should start saving for retirement with money from his or her first paycheck. The power of compounding of interest and investment returns alone creates a compelling reason to start as early as possible.

That is not to say, however, that middle-aged people who have not saved a lot are doomed to retire into poverty. Even a "runway" of as few as fifteen years can produce a significant retirement estate if the person is disciplined and diligent about saving for retirement. Hence, the recommendation to start conversations about retirement planning as early as age fifty or fifty-five.

Recognize that retirement and end-of-career issues can be quite emotional, and be prepared to deal with emotions in a positive and creative way.

So often, I hear an older partner complaining that the younger partners are "kicking me to the curb after all my years with the firm." It doesn't have to be that way. Older partners have to face certain facts, namely these:

- You will not be able to live and practice law forever.
- As you age, you eventually lose a little of your edge and become more prone to making mistakes or forgetting to perform key tasks.
- You cannot predict your death, unless you decide to end your own life.
- You cannot predict whether or when you may become disabled.
- If you want to leave a legacy behind in the form of a continuing law firm that you helped to create, you must have a plan for transitioning ownership to a new generation and transitioning client relationships to that new generation.
- It is in your own best interest to take a leadership role in pressing the succession issue. Far better for you to lead than to have your partners do it for you.
- As you get older, the decisions that will shape your firm's future will have increasingly little impact on you. At some point in time, your views will become irrelevant because it is no longer your future at stake but that of the next generation.
- No law firm ever became a going concern without passing ownership and control to a younger generation. If you resist succession and change, you run the risk that your firm will be relegated to the pile of other "one-generation" law firms.

The succeeding generation of partners also has facts to face:

- Retirement and end-of-career issues are emotionally difficult for those facing them.
- Proper planning and execution of succession is ultimately your responsibility. It is unfair and unwise to leave the whole process up to the retiring partner.
- There is no substitute for frequent, candid, and empathetic conversations about retirement and succession. These conversations should begin early enough to craft an orderly plan and should continue regularly until the transition is complete.

- It is reasonable for a founding partner to expect some remuneration for his or her lifetime investment in creating, growing, and sustaining the law firm.
- Even retired people sometimes want to continued involvement in work at some level. Consider Emeritus plans or counsel status that can provide some continuing work and rewards for former equity partners.
- Once succession is complete, you will now be owners of a new institution that you can shape to conform to your vision. You have a responsibility to make sure that vision includes plans for your own eventual succession. It's in your future, so start planning now.

Make Sure that Succession Planning Includes Personal Planning for the Individual.

Succession planning at the individual level cannot be done without integrating it into financial, retirement, estate, health, and "eldering" planning. Most law firms leave all this up to the individual partner, generally because they believe that these "personal" matters do not affect the life of the firm. Yet, consider what happens when an older partner has not properly prepared for his or her retirement. The most embarrassing situation is one in which a partner has to inform the firm's co-owners that he or she cannot afford to retire and needs to continue to work.

Consequently, well-managed law firms encourage their partners to plan carefully for life's contingencies. From the firm's point of view, the essential planning revolves around making sure that clients can continue to be served if something untoward happens to a partner or key business handler. Of course, this is especially important for solo practitioners and very small firms. That said, even larger firms need to consider how to make sure that multiple lawyers in the firm are familiar with the affairs of important clients.

From a personal planning perspective, law firms also need to make sure that partners are being responsible when it comes to handling their own financial affairs. This is where things get tricky. Where does one draw the line between personal finances and contingencies that might adversely affect the firm or client relationships?

At the very least, firms of anything more than two lawyers should have a practice of discussing candidly and openly the individual retirement goals of the partners. How long do they expect/want to practice law? Do they think they will need a "scale-down" period to prepare for retirement? What are their expectations of the firm after they slow down and/or cease to practice? Do they feel that they are personally prepared financially and emotionally for retirement?

This does not have to happen every year, but it needs to happen. Older partners, especially those who control significant business, do a disservice to the younger partners by not being candid. By the same token, younger partners need to be sensitive to the emotional issues surrounding retirement and end-of-career issues. The older partners should not be made to feel that the next generation partners are circling the boat waiting for them to jump out. However, at some point, critical planning and decision making have to become the responsibility of the younger generation, if the firm is to survive and prosper. If a firm waits too long to deal frankly with these issues, the succession problem can become an existential one. Either the older partners continue to hang on and the younger partners go elsewhere or they find a way to transition the business in an orderly manner to the next generation.

Appendix A

ADOPTING A TWO-TIER PARTNERSHIP— A SUCCESSFUL APPROACH

PETER A. GIULIANI
Smock Law Firm Consultants
Weston, CT

Note: Portions of this white paper have appeared in The American Lawyer *and The American Lawyer Management Service.*[1]

Law practice is perhaps the only remaining large business based upon the notion that compensation and ownership must go hand in hand. In our largest firms, young lawyers have been taught to believe that partnership is the ultimate objective—the sine qua non of their careers. They are also indoctrinated by the "up-or-out" system into believing that success is binary—either you make partner or you are nothing.

The old system, however, is gradually changing. Those entrusted with managing and governing our law businesses are recognizing that for most firms "up-or-out" is, as Irving Shapiro called it, "an act of insanity from a management standpoint." Given today's high cost of recruiting and training top quality associates, few firms can afford to spend seven or eight years developing an excellent lawyer only to jettison him because he failed to survive the cut on schedule.

The enormous salary hikes of the 1980s and the intensifying pressure on the old idea that "leverage equals profits" are forcing firms to reconsider the traditional associate/partner career path. According to Shapiro, "The management issues are exactly the same [as between corporations and law firms]: how to manage without stifling [exceptional talent] and how to get [talented lawyers] to see themselves as an important part of a larger organization to which they have responsibilities." Stated alternatively, the issue is, "How do we preserve our extensive investment in trained and talented lawyers without having to give them all ownership positions in the business?"

Lately, many law firms that have historically adhered to a single-class partnership concept are evaluating two-tier structures as a way to retain high-quality associates who have not otherwise demonstrated equity-partner capabilities. As one partner in a large Chicago firm put it, "If we can make someone an 'income partner' after five years, we have probably forestalled his succumbing to the lure of partnership elsewhere—at least until we have had the chance to evaluate how well he might perform as an 'equity partner.'"

Others are considering using the two-tier structure to fix perceived inequities in the firm's compensation system by creating several classes of nonpercentage "fixed income," or "guaranteed income" partners. Still others use nonequity status to accommodate partners who are "scaling down" to retirement.

The two-tier partnership has been around a long time and has existed in many forms. Some firms have traditionally held all newly admitted partners in a nonequity status for two or three years before elevating them automatically to equity status. Many others, Chicago firms in particular, have had a permanent nonequity partnership status almost from the inception of the firm, as have firms in New York, Boston, and Washington, DC.

There are really two forms of two-tier systems. One is a general partnership, in which some partners have fixed-dollar or guaranteed incomes, but retain all of the other characteristics of general partners. The other is a firm with two separate classes of partners: general partners and limited partners.

Despite their apparent longevity and the recent attention paid to them, many newly implemented two-tier systems are doomed to failure because:

- the firm has misperceived the problem it is trying to fix;
- the firm has correctly perceived the problem but has misperceived the appropriateness of a two-tier system to solving the problem; or
- the firm has failed to implement the two-tier system properly.

The first two conditions relate to selecting the proper tool, the third to using the tool properly. This article addresses both issues.

WHAT PROBLEMS DOES A TWO-TIER SYSTEM FIX?

Here are some typical reasons advanced for adopting a two-tier system:

- "Our operating leverage has slipped and we can't afford any more new equity partners."
- "There is not room in our general partnership for many more partners because we already have too many 'service' partners who are not generating any new business."
- "Several associates are coming up through the ranks who are good technicians, but we're not sure what to do with them."
- "Creating a salaried partner tier will allow us to make more money available to compensate top performers."

Adopting a two-tier partnership form may treat some of these symptoms, but very often more directed measures are needed to correct the root problems.

The first problem relates to operating leverage—often misconstrued to mean the ratio of associates (or total lawyers) to partners. The correct definition of *operating leverage* is "the realizable value of all associate hours (or total lawyer hours), divided by the realizable value of all partner hours." Leverage alone will not produce profits. Leverage only works well when both partner hours *and* associate hours are in excess of breakeven. Restricting the equity partner group when hours are weak across the board does not fix the real problem, which is too many lawyers for the volume of business.

The second problem relates to a lack of effective marketing and business development. It is the age-old problem of too many partners for the amount of work available. Both this problem and the first are more appropriately corrected through a partner goal-setting and accountability program that emphasizes and rewards high-quality business origination, coupled with partner counseling and/or outplacement. Other effective techniques for dealing with these two problems are extending the "track" to partner, raising and enforcing admission standards, and any other artifice that reduces the size of the eye of the needle through which associates must pass to become members of the firm.

If a firm implements a two-tier system to address the third problem, it runs the risk of diluting the meaning of partnership. A two-tier partnership certainly makes it easier to outplace lawyers who eventually don't measure up. It also is a great way to deal with top-performing technicians who are essential to the firm but presently lack a sufficient "book of business" to become equity partners.

Without clearly defined standards as to the significance of partnership status, however, it becomes all too easy to admit and grant tenure to nonequity partners, many of whom will not measure up to anything other than journeyman associate standards. Loading a nonequity tier with average performers will eventually turn it into a "leper colony," while the most interesting and challenging work will gravitate to the best associates.

The fourth problem relates properly to the partner compensation system. One does not need to create a two-tier partnership to fix compensation inequities, although most two-tier partnerships exist for precisely that reason. An alternate and very effective remedy is to deal specifically and directly with performance expectations and compensation within the existing partnership framework. The solution may involve putting some partners on fixed compensation, but that can hardly be construed as implementing a two-tier partnership. It is really a two-tier *compensation system* and not a two-tier *partnership*. While the two-tier partnership deals very effectively with compensation inequities, it is important to remember that compensation is one of several areas affected by a two-tier partnership. If compensation is the only problem needing attention, a two-tier partnership proposal may open up many other issues, which the partnership may not be prepared to address.

Here are the real objectives addressed by the two-tier partnerships:

- retaining of high-quality associates by offering them an alternative career path
- reducing unwanted attrition at the top end of the associate ranks by creating the opportunity to offer (nonequity) partnership status *earlier*
- affording the firm more time to evaluate how lawyers will perform as partners
- retaining long-term voting control of the firm by an ownership group most capable of managing and developing the firm's business

Virtually all other issues are best dealt with by addressing them directly, rather than obliquely through a device like the two-tier partnership. Compensation, operating leverage, quality control, and standards for admission are "gut issues" in their own right. Partner evaluation, motivation, and compensation also stand alone, but clearly are related to partnership structure.

SUCCESSFULLY IMPLEMENTING A TWO-TIER PARTNERSHIP

Moving to a two-tier system from the all-equity form of partnership is not a simple process, especially when such a change requires a supermajority vote of the partners. In some cases, the complexity of the approval process or a lack of solid consensus for change may mean a low likelihood of passing a two-tier resolution. In such situations, the law firm would be well-advised to try to accomplish its objectives through some other vehicle, such as a multitrack compensation system, a career associate position, an outplacement program for clearly underperforming partners, a partner goal-setting and peer review program, etc.

Once a firm has decided to move from an all-equity to a two-tier partnership, there are many structural issues and other matters to be resolved and much planning work to be done to ensure successful transition and achievement of objectives. Whatever the reason for considering a two-tier partnership, there are several preconditions for success:

- The firm must have defined and clearly articulated the objectives it wants to achieve by adopting a two-tier structure, and those objectives must be consistent with the broader objectives articulated in the firm's long-range business plan.
- Some effort should be made in advance to measure firm consensus for adopting a two-tier structure and to sample partner attitudes, opinions, and preferences relative to details of implementation. The resulting structure should reflect the desires of a broad consensus of the partners.
- There must be a strong commitment on the part of the firm to make nonequity partnership a desirable and professionally rewarding status. Nonequity status should not come to mean "second-rate."
- Before adopting a two-tier system, the firm must have reached a consensus on its standards for admission to *both* partner classes. Presumably there are reasons for creating a distinction among partners, and those differentiating reasons must be clearly articulated if there is to be a fair and forthright discussion of the merits of the program.
- Partners must be willing to give the program enthusiastic support, especially when explaining it to associates.

Above all, the firm's overriding concern should be to preserve the quality and integrity of the *equity* partnership. Performance standards for equity partners should be considerably higher than for nonequity partners. And standards for nonequity partners should be considerably higher than for associates.

There are a number of other choices the firm must make in setting up a two-tier partnership, among them:

- What form nonequity partner compensation will take and how the nonequity system relates to the equity system;
- whether nonequity partnership will be a permanent position or an intermediate step on the track to eventual equity partnership;
- whether current equity partners may be considered for reclassification to nonequity status;
- the advisability of grandfathering one or more classes of current associates;
- whether or not nonequity partners will be required to make a cash capital contribution or to purchase inventory values;
- the extent to which general and professional liability will extend to partners of nonequity status;
- voting rights of nonequity partners;
- whether or not there will be different provisions for removal, withdrawal, and retirement of nonequity partners;
- expectations and performance requirements for nonequity partners;
- the extent to which nonequity partners have access to the firm's financial information and data on individual partners' compensation;
- the availability of additional perquisites for nonequity partners relative to associates and equity partners.

COMPENSATION STRUCTURE

The first consideration in planning for a two-tier system is the determination of how nonequity partners are to be compensated and how their compensation system relates to the system for equity partners. Ideally, the system should provide the ability to

- compensate nonequity partners as a group relative to their contribution to the firm's financial results;
- reflect multiple levels of experience and seniority within the nonequity group;

- reward exceptional individual performance in a given year, but not lock in the reward for future years by increasing base compensation; and
- reinforce a sense of mutual cooperation and partnership, both within the nonequity group and the partnership as a whole.

The options below are in use in a number of firms.

OPTIONS	ADVANTAGES	DISADVANTAGES
• Fixed monthly salary or draw	• Compensation is known and fixed in advance of the year • Creates the greatest upside leverage for the equity partners	• No way to reward exceptional performance in a given year • Implies that nonequity partners are more like associates or at least like contract partners
• Fixed monthly salary or draw, plus year-end ad hoc dollar bonus	• Provides a device for rewarding exceptional performance in any one year • Retains upside leverage for equity partners	• Some may come to expect a bonus as a matter of course • Paying some bonus to each partner dilutes the value of the bonus as a reward
• Fixed monthly salary or draw, plus year-end bonus as percentage of firm profits	• Ties bonus to firm financial results • Creates a greater sense of "partnership" between the two partner groups because profits are shared from a common pool	• Same disadvantages as dollar bonus • Dilutes upside leverage of equity partners
• Percentage share with maximum dollar cap	• Same advantages as profit-share bonus • Ties entire compensation to firm results without being overly generous in exceptionally good years	• May be unfairly harsh in a "down" year • Very difficult to administer, especially for multiple levels within nonequity tier
• Percentage share of a separate profit pool	• Similar to percentage share with dollar cap, but uses separate pool for non-equity partner • Affords greater flexibility by allowing equity partners to fix the aggregate share of profits to go to nonequity partners	• May reinforce separation between two classes of partners, because of separate pools • Does not allow for differential compensation for exceptional individual performance

Of course many variations on these basic themes appear among the many individual two-tier structures. There is no perfect system. The best ones retain considerable upside leverage for equity partners, while affording some flexibility for rewarding exceptional individual performance and fostering an internally cooperative spirit.

INTERMEDIATE STEP OR PERMANENT POSITION

An important issue is whether nonequity status will be permanent. A related issue is whether all new partners will be required to serve a term as nonequity partner before being considered for equity status.

There have evolved two recognized forms of two-tier partnership: one in which nonequity status serves as an interim step in the eventual progression to full equity status, and another in which nonequity status functions as a permanent career position. Each has evolved to satisfy different objectives.

The first form serves as a holding ground for "on-track" partner candidates who are eventually expected to reach equity status. It satisfies the objectives of extending the time available to evaluate candidates and improving operating leverage. The second form serves as a permanent career position for high-quality technicians, "service" partners, or good lawyers who do not meet all the qualifications of an equity partner but are worth keeping. This is clearly an alternative career track aimed at retaining high-quality, trained lawyers; improving operating leverage; and preventing long-term dilution of voting control of the firm. While some may eventually make it to equity status, the presumption is that nonequity partnership is a long-term, if not permanent, position.

It is conceivable that a firm could have both forms, in essence creating *three* tiers: equity partner, "on-track" nonequity partner, and permanent nonequity partner. In fact, one firm has created a *fourth* status by requiring all equity partners to step down to nonequity status during the five years immediately before they attain mandatory retirement age.

Multiple tracks are possible within the nonequity tier—just as many all-equity partnerships contain partners of varying rank and status—but they can also be quite confusing to those in the nonequity tier. Like most highly motivated professionals, lawyers like to measure themselves against others in what they perceive to be their peer group. A nonequity partnership with four different peer groups in one class can become counterproductive, particularly for the "on-track" partners biding their time until they become "real" partners.

The ultimate choice is probably dictated by market conditions. In Chicago and Boston, for example, it is more common for all partners to be first admitted to nonequity status and for many, though not all, to eventually become equity partners. A multiple-track nonequity tier will probably work in those cities. In New York, Los Angeles, and San Francisco, however, a formal two-tier partnership is a relatively new phenomenon, and "up-or-out" is still very much the rule. In these and other competitive markets, a firm should probably continue to admit the very best associates directly into the equity ranks rather than putting them in the same bag with lesser cherries where they will stand out by comparison and be easier to pick.

RECLASSIFICATION OF CURRENT EQUITY PARTNERS

Any discussion of converting from all-equity to two-tier partnership form invariably encompasses a debate on whether existing equity partners will be exempt from reclassification to nonequity status, voluntarily or otherwise. As a practical matter, it may be necessary to exempt some or all of the equity partners from possible reclassification as an expedient to getting the two-tier proposal passed. Doing so is at best a "seeming expedient," and firms that put off dealing with the inevitable tough questions should be prepared to suffer the long-term consequences.

No partnership selection process is perfect. Some err on the side of being too restrictive and occasionally fail to recognize someone who is partner material, especially if the associate is a late bloomer. More err on the side of not being selective enough. Consequently, there is almost always a group of partners (one hopes a minority) that feels threatened by a proposal to institute a two-tier partnership.

It is unwise to use a newly implemented two-tier system as an excuse to defrock the disenfranchised. One of the principal benefits, however, to be derived from going to a two-tier system is the opportunity to strengthen and upgrade the quality of the *equity* partnership over the long term. Ideally, it happens in two ways: late bloomers get a chance to come of age in the nonequity tier, and the firm deals humanely with equity partners who are unable to keep pace with their peers. It is far easier, both for the firm *and* the partner in question, to reclassify a partner than to seek his or her resignation. Exempting current partners from reclassification ultimately defers the realization of the "upgrade" benefit far into the future, and leaves only outplacement as a method for dealing with chronic underperformers.

Conversion to two-tier partnership works best when combined with partner self-evaluation, goal setting, and peer review. The firm should define and clearly communicate to the partners the performance expectations for both nonequity and equity partners, along with the standards for admission to each tier. Existing equity partners should assess their own individual performance relative to the firm's expectations and, with the guidance of the firm's leaders, prepare personal development plans for achieving or maintaining an appropriate level of performance. Chronic underperformers should be counseled and given a period of time (anywhere from six months to two years, depending upon individual circumstances and roles in the firm) to achieve a reasonable performance standard. Those failing to make the grade within the allotted time, after adjustments in compensation to reflect their undercontribution, should be asked to accept nonequity status as an alternative to leaving the firm.

GRANDFATHERING ASSOCIATES

Many firms are in a similar quandary over whether certain classes of associates should be grandfathered from consideration for nonequity partnership. When some firms recruited associate lawyers, they may have created the expectation that they would have one class of partners forever. Grandfathering associates is perceived as a way to deal with what these firms mistakenly consider to be a broken promise.

Twenty-five years ago, a law firm could promise recruits that, if they stayed with the firm the requisite number of years and continued to perform to a high standard of technical excellence, they would become equity partners. But law firms are no different from any other business enterprise. Times change, and firms must change with them to survive. The compensation increases, intensified competition, and firm realignments of the 1980s have made it impossible for law firms to live up to an expectation that equity partnership is a matter of time and grade or that partnership structures will remain constant forever.

Associates realize this, and many would prefer to trade the "up-or-out" system for a two-tier partnership. In several questionnaire surveys of very large law firms, the overwhelming majority (more than 75 percent) of associates believed that a two-tier partnership was inevitable for their firms and that it also was a *highly desirable* innovation. Associates read the same trade papers that partners read and are well aware that what Steven Brill calls "supply-side growth" is a phenomenon of the past, that competition for partnership slots will intensify, and that firms will ultimately have to adopt alternative career paths (e.g., two-tier partnerships, career associate positions, etc.) to protect their investments in experienced talent. Many associates, weary of the competitive pace of "up-or-out" systems but still attracted to the professional challenges of private practice, may welcome the prospect of aspiring to a position of partnership status that requires less of a personal sacrifice to attain. And in any event, associates recognize that it is in their favor to have more career options rather than fewer.

From the firm's point of view, grandfathering associates has the same effect as exempting partners from possible reclassification. Moreover, it perpetuates the "up-or-out" system, which is one of the key problems the two-tier partnership is designed to fix.

CAPITAL CONTRIBUTION

By and large, firms with two-tier partnerships do not require nonequity partners to make cash capital contributions or purchase accrual inventory values (i.e., unbilled and uncollected time and disbursements). In fact, the adjective "nonequity" connotes the absence of ownership and thus implies no capital contribution or "buy-in" should be required.

In some instances, a capital contribution may be required. For example, if a firm maintains a junior-partner class from which all members are expected to eventually reach full equity status, a modest capital assessment may be made each year as an advance contribution toward the buy-in that the partner will ultimately be required to make. Firms that are professional corporations and create the nonequity class by issuing preferred or Class B common shares may require nonequity class members to purchase shares at some value—a de facto capital contribution.

Whatever the reason for requiring capital contributions from nonequity partners, however modest, the firm will then have to consider several other questions, such as the following:

- Will the contribution be required in a lump sum or in several installments? Will it be withheld from salaries or draws?
- Should the firm provide for bank financing of the contribution?
- Will nonequity partners' capital accounts earn interest? Will the firm charge interest on capital account deficiencies?
- Will nonequity partners' capital accounts have a preferred payout position if the firm dissolves?

For the most part, it is probably desirable to exempt nonequity partners from capital assessments. It is clearly simpler, for both accounting and tax purposes, to require capital only from equity partners

EXTENT OF LIABILITY

The question of professional and general liability of nonequity partners is perhaps the most controversial and toughest to resolve. The general public almost certainly has the right to expect that a lawyer who calls himself a "partner," and whose firm also uses the title, is jointly and severally liable with all other partners of the firm in matters of both general and professional liability. Yet the nonequity partner might argue, "How can you hold me liable for the downside risk of liability without affording me the upside benefits of ownership, not to mention a vote in partnership matters?"

One way of dealing with the liability question is to treat *all* partners as *general* partners. Make it clear to the nonequity partner—and so provide in the firm's partnership agreement—that he or she, along with all other partners, is both jointly and severally liable. Dissenters can remain career associates or leave the firm.

An alternative is to set up a limited partnership to cover nonequity status. Provide in the firm's partnership agreement that liability extends to only the general partners, and that the equity partners will indemnify nonequity partners from any and all general or professional liability claims.

For many reasons, not the least of which is a well-founded ethical concern for preserving public confidence in the profession, some firms have chosen to extend full liability to all partners regardless of status. They have undoubtedly encountered recalcitrant associates who balked at accepting full liability along with nonequity status. Difficult as it may be to lose high-quality lawyers, the firm must be willing to cut loose those who will not accept full liability.

The limited partnership approach is probably easier to deal with internally. If the firm chooses the limited partnership route, there are at least three "stakeholders" that the firm should immediately inform regarding the new arrangement: the insurance carrier, the landlord, and the firm's banker(s).

VOTING RIGHTS

In discussing voting rights, one has to make the distinction between opinion surveys and binding votes of the partnership. Depending upon the decision at hand, it may be advisable to solicit opinions from all partners and associates before making a final decision or putting a motion before the partnership. Such consensus building is helpful in sorting out subsidiary issues and necessary to solidify and document management's mandate, especially in possibly unpopular decisions. This discussion is not concerned with consensus building but rather with binding votes under the terms of the partnership agreement.

As a general rule, nonequity partners should have greater voice and participation in firm management than associates, especially to emphasize the distinction between associate and partner status and add credibility to the nonequity partner position. Most firms that have created two-tier systems, however, did so to prevent dilution of equity partner voting interests. Accordingly, most exclude nonequity partners from binding votes, although the better-managed ones are careful to solicit views of nonequity partners before the binding vote is taken. This is the "cleanest" sort of system and is preferable to diluting voting interests of the real owners of the firm.

While very few firms, if any, extend full voting rights (one partner, one vote) to nonequity partners, some may elect to grant modified voting rights to the nonequity group. The partnership agreement should be clear about the circumstances under which nonequity partners may vote (e.g., upon the admission of new nonequity partners) and about the significance of the outcome of their voting (e.g., counts as the equivalent of one equity partner's vote in the final election). The firm may also allow voting by nonequity partners, but limit the weight given to their vote vis-à-vis equity partners.

REMOVAL, WITHDRAWAL, AND RETIREMENT PROVISIONS

In its broadest sense, partnership means mutual risk taking and shared rewards for team efforts in which all partners pull together. The reality is, of course, that not all partners contribute in proportion to their share of the reward. In addition, partnership admission processes are not perfect. Many firms have equity partners within their ranks who should not have been made partners. The challenge facing many firms is how to correct past mistakes without upsetting the traditional partnership culture.

Few firms today can continue to operate on the premise that partnership involves lifetime tenure. In all but the most "Olympian" firms, outplacement of chronic underperformers is becoming a necessary option for firm leaders who seek to preserve the firm's profitability and franchise. As a result, partnership agreements are affording more leeway in removal of partners, equity and nonequity alike.

Removal of an equity partner usually involves a forced voluntary withdrawal, unless the removal is an expulsion for cause. While most partnership agreements provide for an appeal procedure in the event a partner is asked to leave, few, if any, invoke the right to submit the removal to a vote.

There is a prevailing notion that equity partnership should carry considerably more tenure than nonequity status. Consequently, removal of a nonequity partner generally is—and should be—much easier to accomplish. In most two-tier partnerships, removal of a nonequity partner is simply a matter of management consensus and is implemented without right of appeal by the nonequity partner.

The two-tier partnership offers firm management an alternative to forced withdrawal as a means for dealing with chronic underperformers. Some equity partners may be asked to accept nonequity status voluntarily instead of leaving the firm altogether. In many cases, accepting reduced performance expectations and commensurate rewards is far preferable to forced resignation. The partner may also find that a nonequity partnership affords all the professional status the partnership implies, without the stress of having to keep pace with other equity partners to justify a percentage share of the pie.

EXPECTATIONS AND PERFORMANCE REQUIREMENTS

Nonequity partnership should have a status and cachet all its own if it is to be a meaningful distinction. There is a great temptation to use the position merely as a dumping ground for people who have not made the grade but who would be "inconvenient" to lose. Nonequity status should not be cheapened by using it as a way for the firm to avoid the possibly unpleasant task of telling an associate why he or she is not being admitted. The position should be one of distinction, and those who achieve it should be recognized. They should also be given clearly defined performance objectives, which reflect a higher standard than those for associates, and asked to develop personal development plans for achieving them.

For most firms, nonequity status is not necessarily permanent. Virtually all two-tier partnerships provide for a nonequity partners to be admitted to equity status when or if they have demonstrated, through consistent performance, that they can meet equity-partner standards. It is important, therefore, to spell out clearly the performance expectations for both levels of partner and build them into a partner goal-setting and performance evaluation system.

One of the important benefits derived from adopting a two-tier partnership is the opportunity to establish a slower and more selective "track" for admission to equity status for those lawyers who need more time to develop. Firms that establish a second timetable for nonequity partners lose this important benefit by setting up another career milestone, the outcome of which is binary—either one "makes it" within three years or one "fails." It is important that admission of a nonequity partner to equity partnership occurs when the lawyer is considered ready, and not according to some time-and-grade schedule.

ACCESS TO FINANCIAL INFORMATION

One should start with the general premise that information on firm finances is best restricted to the owners of the business, namely the equity partners, unless a compelling argument can be made for sharing such information. Information on the compensation of individual partners should most certainly be restricted to the equity partner group. In fact, some firms restrict access to compensation data to the firm's executive or compensation committees.

Concerns about the need for confidentiality in compensation matters notwithstanding, a firm that bars nonequity partners from access to firm-wide financials robs them—and the firm—of an important professional development experience. In most cases, all partners, both equity and nonequity, should have regular and timely access to firm-wide financial statements and performance reports for major operating units (i.e., practice areas, offices, etc.). While nonequity partners are not considered "at risk," they are, nevertheless, an important component of the partnership and will probably never develop the entrepreneurial skills required for equity status without the valuable learning experience of wrestling with and using firm financial information as a management tool.

PERKS RELATIVE TO ASSOCIATES AND EQUITY PARTNERS

Nonequity status should carry with it certain trappings that distinguish the position from associate status and communicate that distinction to others in the firm. Differential compensation, performance expectations, and access to information are ways to reinforce the new nonequity partner's awareness of the status differential. New privileges and perquisites are ways to reinforce the distinction outwardly to others in the firm.

Some typical externally distinguishing attributes and "perks" include:

- use of the title "partner";
- full-time secretaries, or at least a greater share of a secretary;
- larger offices than those for associates—possibly even equivalent to those for equity partners;
- firm-paid luncheon club memberships;
- greater responsibilities in the firm's recruiting and training programs;
- participation and possibly leadership positions in firm committees;
- recognized supervisory roles in complex matters; and
- greater responsibilities for evaluating associate performance.

There are many other distinguishing characteristics and privileges of rank a firm might offer. The important point is that nonequity partner status should be made to appear and feel different from associate status. Attaining the position of nonequity partner should be considered a career milestone and not a side step into a dead end.

CONCLUSION

Many reasons have been advanced for adopting a two-tier partnership structure. Perhaps the most important reasons are to protect the firm's investment in legal talent and to streamline firm decision making. Perceived compensation inequities can be addressed within traditional partnership forms but generally are much easier to manage within the context of a two-tier partnership.

It is a very tricky process to move from the traditional all-equity form to a two-tier partnership without upsetting key "stakeholders"—associates and partners alike. If it is properly managed and implemented sensitively, the transition to a two-tier partnership can be a healthy experience, especially if the new position is well defined and attaining it is regarded by associates and partners alike as a significant career milestone. It is very important, however, to do one's homework on consensus building and to do a lot of communicating before attempting to force the issue.

Appendix B

POLICY ON RETIREMENT OF PARTNERS AND "PARTNER EMERITUS" STATUS

1. Each Equity Partner in the firm shall have the opportunity to change his or her status to that of a "Partner Emeritus," solely at the his or her option, on each January 1st after the Partner reaches age sixty through and including the January 1st after the Partner reaches age seventy. In this regard, each Partner, at his or her annual peer review, which occurs in October of each year, will discuss with the Partner conducting the peer review his or her future plans with respect to continuing to practice law at the firm, including plans relating to election of Partner Emeritus status.
2. Any Partner who wants to change his or her status to that of Partner Emeritus or retain Partner Emeritus status after he or she attains the age of seventy-one must submit a request to the Partnership, and that request must be approved by the Partnership.
3. Upon becoming a Partner Emeritus, (i) the Partner shall receive payment of his or her capital account in accordance with terms of the Partnership Agreement; (ii) the amount of the Partner's past service compensation will become fixed and be payable in accordance with the terms of the Partnership Agreement; (iii) the Partner shall become of counsel to the firm; (iv) the Partner Emeritus will no longer be a Partner of the firm; and (v) the Partner and the firm will enter into a

mutually acceptable Partner Emeritus Agreement as provided in Paragraph 6 hereof.

4. Several options will be available for continuing the relationship between the firm and a Partner Emeritus. One or more of these options will be agreed upon by the firm and the Partner Emeritus during each fiscal year, commencing with the fiscal year in which a Partner first becomes a Partner Emeritus. The option agreed upon by a Partner Emeritus and the firm for any particular fiscal year shall not be changed during that fiscal year, except upon mutual agreement of the firm and the Partner Emeritus.
5. The options available, upon mutual agreement of the firm and the Partner Emeritus, will include, but not necessarily be limited to the following:

(A) FULL-TIME PRACTICE WITH THE FIRM: The Partner Emeritus may continue to practice law full-time with the firm, be compensated in the same manner as other Partners, and continue to have all the benefits then available to a Partner, including but not limited to office space, secretarial support, associate attorney support, group health insurance, group life insurance, professional liability insurance, bar dues, occupational license fees, reimbursement of club dues, continuing legal education (CLE) budget, a business development budget, firm trips, paid vacations, or as may otherwise be provided from time to time by the firm to its Partners; provided, however, after the Partner Emeritus reaches age seventy, the Partner Emeritus may, at his or her election, continue to have his or her spouse covered under the firm's group health insurance at the firm's expense (if allowed under the terms and provisions of the firm's group health insurance policy then in place) until the date that such spouse is eligible for Medicare coverage or other similar governmental health insurance program. In addition, upon the death of the Partner Emeritus, his or her spouse shall continue to be covered under the firm's group health insurance (if allowed under the terms and provisions of the firm's group health insurance policy then in effect) at the firm's expense until the earlier of (i) the date upon which such spouse is eligible for Medicare coverage or other similar governmental health insurance program (ii) the date upon which such spouse remarries or (iii) that date which is three years after the date of the death of the Partner Emeritus.

(B) PART-TIME PRACTICE WITH THE FIRM: The Partner Emeritus may work part-time, or otherwise carry a reduced workload. In this case, the Partner Emeritus will be compensated either (i) on the same basis as the other Partners, with the understanding that the firm, through its compensation process, will take into consideration the reduced effort and/or productivity, or (ii) on a different basis agreed upon by the firm and the Partner Emeritus, such as, but not necessarily limited to, an hourly payment rate for collected billed hours. Until the Partner Emeritus reaches age seventy, the Partner Emeritus and his or her spouse, if such spouse is covered as of the day Partner Emeritus status is elected, will continue to be covered by the firm's group health insurance and the Partner Emeritus will continue to have group life insurance, coverage under the firm's group policy, all at the firm's expense. After the Partner Emeritus reaches age seventy, the Partner Emeritus shall no longer be entitled to coverage under the firm's group health insurance, but the Partner Emeritus may, at his or her election, (i) continue to have his or her spouse covered under the firm's group health insurance (if allowed under the terms and provisions of the firm's group health insurance coverage then in place) until the date that such spouse is eligible for Medicare coverage or other similar governmental health insurance program; and/or (ii) continue to have group life insurance coverage under the firm's group term life insurance policy, provided that the cost of such continued group health insurance coverage for the spouse of the Partner Emeritus and/or group life insurance coverage for the Partner Emeritus shall be paid by the Partner Emeritus or his or her surviving spouse. The Partner Emeritus will also continue to have reasonable use of an office, an appropriate level of secretarial support, and professional liability insurance coverage. Other benefits, including associate attorney support, bar dues, occupational license fees, reimbursement of club dues, CLE budget, a business development budget, firm trips, paid vacations, etc.,would be tailored to meet the individual situation in the discretion of the firm. In addition, upon the death of the Partner Emeritus, his or her spouse shall continue to be covered under the firm's group health insurance (if allowed under the terms and provisions of the firm's group health insurance policy then in effect) at the firm's expense until the earlier of (i) the date upon which such spouse is eligible for Medicare coverage or other similar governmental health insurance program, (ii) the date upon which such spouse remarries, or (iii) that date which is three years after the date of death of the Partner Emeritus.

(C) RETIREMENT—PERFORMS NO OR NOMINAL LEGAL WORK FOR THE FIRM: The Partner Emeritus may retire and perform no legal work for the firm or its clients, except as provided in Paragraph 11 below. Until the retired Partner Emeritus becomes eligible for Medicare coverage or other similar governmental health insurance program, the retired Partner Emeritus may, at his or her election, (i) continue to be covered by the firm's group health insurance program, (ii) continue to have his or her spouse covered under the firm's group health insurance (if allowed under the terms and provisions of the firm's group health insurance coverage then in place) until the date such spouse is eligible for Medicare coverage or other similar governmental health insurance program, and/or (iii) continue to have group life insurance coverage under the firm's group life coverage, provided that the cost of such continued group health insurance coverage and/or group life insurance coverage shall be paid by the retired Partner Emeritus. The retired Partner Emeritus will continue to have reasonable use of an office, to the extent office space is then available, and an appropriate level of secretarial support. Other benefits, if any, will be determined by the firm in its discretion. At such time as the retired Partner Emeritus and/or his or her spouse shall become eligible for Medicare coverage or other similar governmental health insurance program, neither shall be entitled to continue participation in coverage under the firm group insurance plans and policies, whether at the expense of the firm or at the expense of the retired Partner Emeritus or surviving spouse. In addition, upon the death of the retired Partner Emeritus, his or her spouse shall continue to be covered under the firm's group health insurance (if allowed under the terms and provisions of the firm's group health insurance policy then in effect) at the expense of such surviving spouse until the earlier of (i) the date upon which such spouse is eligible for Medicare coverage or other similar governmental health insurance program, (ii) the date upon which such spouse remarries, or (iii) that date which is three years after the date of death of the retired Partner Emeritus.

6. The option or arrangement mutually agreed upon by any Partner Emeritus and the firm shall be memorialized during each applicable fiscal year in a written Partner Emeritus Agreement, which shall be based upon the firm's standard form of agreement, and shall set forth and include the basic terms of the option or arrangement mutually agreed upon. Such Partner Emeritus Agreement shall incorporate applicable provisions of the firm's Partnership

Agreement, and upon execution of that Partner Emeritus Agreement, the Partnership Agreement then in effect between the firm and that Partner Emeritus will terminate (except for the provisions relating to the payment of past service compensation).

7. Each Partner Emeritus who has elected either option (A) or option (B) under Paragraph 5 of this Policy will be expected to participate in a peer review during each fiscal year to determine how the current arrangement between the Partner Emeritus and the firm is working (for both) and to discuss the arrangement between the Partner Emeritus and the firm for the following fiscal year (which shall be subject to approval as required herein).
8. The year-to-year arrangement between the firm and the Partner Emeritus will be determined each year by mutual agreement of the Partner Emeritus and the firm, provided that for each year after the Partner Emeritus reaches age seventy, any decision of the firm to permit the Partner Emeritus to continue practicing law or otherwise working for the firm and its clients, as well as the terms and provisions of such working arrangement, must be approved by the firm. If such decision and working arrangement are not approved by the firm, the Partner Emeritus will be required to elect the option provided in Paragraph 5(C) above.
9. No Partner Emeritus will be requested or required to execute any individual guaranty or indemnity agreement with respect to any loan obtained by the firm or lease agreement for office space entered into by the firm. In addition, the firm will use its best efforts to have each Partner Emeritus released from any guaranty or indemnity agreement previously executed by that Partner Emeritus. In the event that any particular lender or creditor refuses to release a Partner Emeritus from any particular guaranty or indemnity agreement, each of the other Partners in the firm will execute indemnification and hold harmless agreements in favor of the Partner Emeritus so that the Partner Emeritus will be indemnified and held harmless by them against any further liability or responsibility incurred by the Partner Emeritus under any such unreleased guaranty or indemnity agreement.
10. Each Partner Emeritus will be expected to continue to promote the best interests of the firm and to generally be an "ambassador" for the firm.

Each Partner Emeritus will also be expected, to the fullest extent such Partner Emeritus is reasonably able to do so, to see to the general turnover of clients of such Partner Emeritus to other lawyers in the firm. Such client turnover will be accomplished as part of the slowing down and retiring process, but it will be left to each individual Partner Emeritus as to how client turnover will be handled and ultimately accomplished. In addition, each Partner Emeritus will be expected, when he or she deems it to be appropriate, to prepare a proposal for the transfer of client origination credit (to the extent allowed under the current firm policy) and billing lawyer responsibility within the firm for his or her clients and to submit such proposal to the firm for approval (or modification, as required) and implementation. Wherever possible, such Partner Emeritus should, as appropriate, also encourage the turnover to other lawyers in the firm of directorships, fiduciary positions, community leadership positions, etc.

11. After retirement pursuant to Paragraph 5(C) or Paragraph 8 above, the retired Partner Emeritus will not engage in the practice of law or any activity that involves the provision of legal services to others without first obtaining the approval of the firm. If such approval is not obtained and the retired Partner Emeritus practices law or provides such services, then the remedy of the firm shall be the right to terminate the balance of any unpaidpast service compensation and to otherwise terminate any other benefits then being provided to the retired Partner Emeritus. In reviewing any request from a retired Partner Emeritus for approval of any such activity, the firm shall decide the matter based upon what it determines to be in the long-term best interest of the firm. Examples of activities for a retired Partner Emeritus that could be approved by the firm under appropriate circumstances are the following:
    - (A) conducting mediations or arbitrations
    - (B) performing pro bono legal work
    - (C) teaching at a law school
    - (D) practicing law on a limited basis outside the State of [STATE]
    - (E) becoming a member of the judiciary

12. A Partner Emeritus shall not receive any payment from the firm other than payments contemplated in this Policy; i.e., the compensation agreed to annually, if any, pursuant to the provisions of Paragraph 5

above and the past service compensation payable to that Partner Emeritus by the firm.

13. The firm shall have the right and authority to vary the application of the retirement policy described herein to any particular Partner Emeritus in one or more respects if such variance(s) is (are) agreed upon by that Partner Emeritus and is (are) deemed by the firm to be in the best interest of the firm; except that the provision set forth in Paragraph 8 above requiring firm approval to permit a Partner Emeritus to continue practicing law or otherwise working for the firm and its clients after the Partner Emeritus reaches age seventy may only be changed, amended, or modified pursuant to Paragraph 15 below.

14. With respect to any Partner who decides to either (i) work part-time or otherwise carry a reduced workload or (ii) retire and perform no legal work for the firm or its clients (except as provided in Paragraph 11 above), at a time or under circumstances where such Partner is not eligible for Partner Emeritus status under the firm's Policy but wants to avail himself or herself of the options available to a Partner Emeritus under this Policy, the firm may agree upon an arrangement between such Partner and the firm, similar to the status of Partner Emeritus.

15. This Policy on Retirement of Partners and "Partner Emeritus" Status may only be changed, amended, or modified at any time pursuant to an amendment approved by a vote of the Partners of the firm, except that the provisions relating to past service compensation and the provisions of Paragraph 9 above relating to indemnification of a Partner Emeritus may not be retroactively changed or amended as to any Partner Emeritus without his or her consent.

17. This amended and restated policy on Retirement of Partners and "Partner Emeritus" Status will become effective on the day it is approved and adopted by the firm.

18. When used anywhere in this Policy, the term "spouse" shall mean and include: (i) the person married to the Partner Emeritus or (ii) the person who is in a "domestic partnership" with the Partner Emeritus, as such term is from time to time defined by the insurance company providing group health insurance coverage for the firm and its employees.

Appendix C

SAMPLE LANGUAGE

While this book was never intended to serve as a guide and model form for drafting a law firm retirement plan, I thought it would be helpful to include an example of language that other firms have adopted in their initial partnership agreements. This language, it must be understood, has had no legal review whatsoever and so should be treated as such. Again, the best way to understand the language is in the context of case studies.

Case Study: A New Firm

In this case, two lawyers had been practicing law together for several years under a "handshake" partnership agreement. They decided that they would eventually want to admit new partners and wanted to formalize that process to make it explainable and consistent. They wanted to preserve control for a period of time—long enough to manage the firm the way they wanted to, but not so long that the subject of management succession would become an issue. They also wanted a way to value the firm so that their interests could be gradually bought out by succeeding generations of partners, rather than waiting until retirement to pass along the value of equity.

Following is an example of agreement language that accomplished those goals:

Executive Committee. The principal governing body of the Partnership shall be its Executive Committee, initially composed of the two founding Partners. [Partner A, age sixty] shall serve as Executive Partner for a term of three years and may be elected to a second three-year term. No Executive Partner shall serve beyond the age of sixty-seven.

[Partner B, age fifty-two] shall serve as Managing Partner for a term of three years and may be elected to up to two additional three-year terms. He may also be elected to serve as Executive Partner in the event that the position becomes vacant.

The respective duties and executive functions of the Executive Partner and Managing Partner shall be defined by the Executive Committee.

Additional Executive Committee Members. Other Partners may be appointed to the Executive Committee by unanimous consent of the two founding Partners. Other Partners may be appointed to serve the Partnership in specific roles as defined by the Executive Committee, without being appointed to the Executive Committee.

Full Authority. All Partners hereby cede full authority to govern and manage the Partnership to the Executive Committee. While members of the Executive Committee may consult with other Partners from time to time regarding important firm decisions, they are not bound by the advice and consent of said other Partners in reaching final decisions.

Changes to Governance. This governance arrangement and the relative responsibilities and authority of Partners may be changed only by unanimous consent of the members of the Executive Committee.

Two Classes of Partner. There are two designated classes of Partner: Capital Partner and Income Partner. This Partnership Agreement is intended to bind and govern both Capital and Income Partners.

Capital Partners, Ownership Rights. Capital Partners have the following rights and obligations:

- commercial and professional liability, in accordance with prevailing law governing Limited Liability Partnerships
- an obligation to provide operating capital to finance the business of the Partnership
- ownership of the Firm's net tangible and intangible assets in accordance with ownership percentages, determined herein
- sharing of the profits and losses of the Firm in accordance with income percentages as determined by the Partnership's compensation plan, defined herein
- residual ownership interest, in accordance with ownership percentages, in the net assets of the estate of the Partnership in the event of dissolution
- a vote in the governance of the Firm in accordance with ownership percentages, determined herein
- ability and duty to serve on the Firm's Executive Committee, if appointed
- ability to assume such management roles as may be assigned by the Executive Committee from time to time

Income Partners' Limited Rights and Liability. Income Partners shall have the following limited rights and obligations:

- sharing of the profits and losses of the Firm in accordance with the compensation plan, described herein
- [rofessional liability in accordance with prevailing law governing Limited Liability Partnerships
- indemnification from commercial liability by the Capital Partners
- ability and duty to assume such management roles as may be assigned by the Executive Committee from time to time
- no binding vote in the governance or management of the Partnership or any of its businesses
- no current or residual ownership interest in the tangible and intangible net assets of the Partnership or any of its businesses

Indemnification of Income Partners. The Capital Partners shall indemnify each Income Partner for any losses incurred or judgments entered against the Partnership, except for matters arising from an Income Partner's own malpractice, errors, or omissions.

Admission of New Partners by Simple Majority of Executive Committee. Admission of new Capital Partners and Income Partners requires a simple majority vote of the members of the Executive Committee, voting according to relative ownership percentages, determined herein.

Ownership Percentages. Upon execution of this Agreement, the Partnership will create one thousand ownership shares. Initially, Partner A and Partner B will own five hundred ownership shares each, representing a 50 percent ownership percentage for each Capital Partner. A Capital Partner's ownership percentage shall be the ratio of his or her ownership shares, expressed as a percentage of the total one thousand ownership shares.

Income Partners. Income Partners may not acquire ownership shares in the Partnership but may be invited to become Capital Partners and then acquire ownership shares. As new Capital Partners are admitted, they will be allowed to acquire such number of ownership shares as will be determined by the Partnership's Executive Committee in advance of their admission as Capital Partners.

Admission of New Capital Partners and Acquisition of Ownership Shares. The admission of a new Capital Partner shall be determined by a majority vote of the members of the Partnership's Executive Committee (see above). The Executive Committee shall also determine the number of ownership shares that will be offered to each new **Capital Partner**. From time to time, the Executive Committee may also decide to offer additional ownership shares for acquisition by existing Capital Partners, and in doing so may increase the number of ownership shares outstanding.

Valuation of Ownership Shares. The value of ownership shares for acquisition purposes shall be determined annually as of December 31 in accordance with the following methodology:

Cash Net Assets

The Partnership's independent accountants shall determine the value of cash-basis net assets of the Partnership as of December 31, in accordance with cash-basis principles of accounting.

The cash value of each ownership share shall be then determined by dividing the value of cash-basis net assets by 1,000, or the number of ownership shares outstanding.

New Capital Partners will acquire their ownership shares by tendering an amount of cash equal to the number of shares being acquired times the cash value, as determined above.

Accrual Net Assets

The Executive Committee, in consultation with the Firm's independent accountants, shall agree upon a fair value for the Partnership's uncollected accounts receivable (fees) and unbilled work in progress (fees). Such valuation shall take into account the following factors:

- the balances of the Partnership's accounts for accounts receivable and unbilled work in progress, as recorded in the Partnership's timekeeping and billing system
- the percentage of unbilled and uncollected accounts that are likely to eventually prove uncollectible (i.e., allowance for doubtful accounts)
- the net realizable value of any matters or cases that are being handled on a contingency-fee basis

The accrual value of each ownership share shall be then determined by dividing the value of accrual net assets by 1,000, or the number of ownership shares outstanding.

New Capital Partners will acquire their ownership shares in either of or a combination of two ways:

- forgoing future compensation otherwise payable under the Partnership's compensation plan in an amount equal to the number of shares being acquired times the accrual value, as determined above; (Note: This amount may be prorated, with the approval of the Executive Committee over a future period not to exceed five years.)
- pledging accounts receivable due from their own clients for work they performed for such clients prior to becoming Capital Partners.

Annual Revaluation Each year, the ownership shares shall be revalued as of December 31, in consultation with the Firm's independent accountants, and each Capital Partner's individual ownership interest in the three classes of net assets shall be determined and recorded by the Partnership.

Appendix D BIBLIOGRAPHY AND OTHER USEFUL RESOURCES

American Bar Association Resources

American Bar Association. "Senior Lawyers Division." http://www.americanbar.org/groups/senior_lawyers.html (accessed March 19, 2013).

American Bar Association. *Model Rules of Professional Conduct*. Chicago: American Bar Association, 2012.

Aspinwall, Marla J., and Michael G. Goldstein. *Taxation and Funding of Nonqualified Deferred Compensation*. Chicago: American Bar Association, 2012.

Berson, Susan A. *The Lawyer's Retirement Planning Guide*. Chicago: American Bar Association, 2009.

Dickie, Robert B. *Financial Statement Analysis and Business Valuation for the Practical Lawyer*. 2nd ed. Chicago: American Bar Association, 2006.

Gallagher, Stephen P., Edward H. Flitton III, and Mary Cranston. "Retirement Planning for Senior Lawyers: How to Structure a Retirement Program So That Senior Lawyers Transition to Retirement in a Fulfilling Manner without Undue Cost to the Rest of the Firm." Paper presented at the annual meeting of the American Bar Association, San Francisco, August 2007.

Munneke, Gary A., and Anthony E. Davis. *The Essential Formbook: Comprehensive Management Tools for Lawyers*. Vol. 1, *Partnership and Organizational Agreements/Client Intake and Fee Agreements*. Chicago: American Bar Association, 2003.

Munneke, Gary A., and Anthony E. Davis. *The Essential Formbook: Comprehensive Management Tools for Lawyers*. Vol. 2, *Human Resources/Fees, Billing, and Collection*. Chicago: American Bar Association, 2001.

Munneke, Gary A., and Anthony E. Davis. *The Essential Formbook: Comprehensive Management Tools for Lawyers*. Vol. 3, *Calendar, Docket, and File Management/Law Firm Financial Analysis*. Chicago: American Bar Association, 2003.

Munneke, Gary A., and Anthony E. Davis. *The Essential Formbook: Comprehensive Management Tools for Lawyers*. Vol. 4, *Disaster Planning and Recovery/Risk Management and Professional Liability Insurance*. Chicago: American Bar Association, 2001.

Risius, Jeffrey M. *Business Valuation: A Primer for the Legal Profession*. Chicago: American Bar Association, 2007.

Rothschild, Lowell E., comp., and Edward B. Berger, ed. *Withdrawal, Retirement & Disputes: What You and Your Firm Need to Know*. Chicago: American Bar Association, 1986.

Skoloff, Gary N., and Theodore P. Orenstein. *When a Lawyer Divorces: How to Value a Professional Practice*. Chicago: American Bar Association, 1986.

Wren, Harold G., and Beverly J. Glascock. *The Of Counsel Agreement: A Guide for Law Firm and Practitioner*. 3rd ed. Chicago: American Bar Association, 2005.

New York State Bar Association Resources

Burke, Walter T., and Timothy E. Casserly. "Retirement: The End or the Beginning." *The Senior Lawyer* 3, no. 1 (Fall 2011).

Giuliani, Peter A. *Model Partnership Agreements for New York Law Firms*. New York State Bar Association, 2008.

Giuliani, Peter A., and Walter T. Burke. *Selling Your Law Practice: A Program for Solo and Small Firm Practitioners*. New York State Bar Association, 2012. Video webcast archive.

Jackson, Barry E., Roseann S. Lentin, Gary A. Munneke, and Kimberly A. Swetland. *Best Practices in Legal Management: A Comprehensive Guide*. New York State Bar Association, 2010.

New York State Bar Association Special Commission on Age Discrimination in the Profession. *Report and Recommendations on Mandatory Retirement Practices in the Profession.* New York State Bar Association, 2007.

Other Resources

Brennan, William F. "Law Firm Valuation, Parts I, II, and III." Altman Weil, 2010.

Business Valuation Law News. "Ten Steps to Value Law Firm Contingency Cases." March 11, 2010 http://www.bvlawnews.com/goodwill/ten-steps-to-value-law-firm-contingency-cases/

Shapiro, Irving. "Running a People Business." *The American Lawyer,* September 1989.

Smock, John S. "Dealing with Underperforming Partners – At the Top of Every Managing Partner's *To Do* List." Smock Law Firm Consultants, 2012.

http://www.smocklawfirmconsultants.com/images/Dealing_with_Underproductive_Partners_(Sept_2012).pdf

Trugman, Gary R. *Understanding Business Valuation: A Practical Guide to Valuing Small to Medium Sized Businesses.* 4th ed. American Institute of Certified Public Accountants, 2012.

Weisman, Mary-Lou. "The History of Retirement, From Early Man to A.A.R.P." *The New York Times,* March 21, 1999.

Wilkins, David B. "Partner, Shmartner! EEOC v. Sidley Austin Brown & Wood." *Harvard Law Review* 120, (2007).

Index

E

F

G

H

I

J

L

M

N

O

Virtual Law Practice: How to Deliver Legal Services Online

By Stephanie L. Kimbro

Product Code: 5110707 • **LPM Price:** $47.95 • **Regular Price:** $79.95

The legal market has recently experienced a dramatic shift as lawyers seek out alternative methods of practicing law and providing more affordable legal services. Virtual law practice is revolutionizing the way the public receives legal services and how legal professionals work with clients. If you are interested in this form of practicing law, *Virtual Law Practice* will help you:

- Responsibly deliver legal services online to your clients
- Successfully set up and operate a virtual law office
- Establish a virtual law practice online through a secure, client-specific portal
- Manage and market your virtual law practice
- Understand state ethics and advisory opinions
- Find more flexibility and work/life balance in the legal profession

Social Media for Lawyers: The Next Frontier

By Carolyn Elefant and Nicole Black

Product Code: 5110710 • **LPM Price:** $47.95 • **Regular Price:** $79.95

The world of legal marketing has changed with the rise of social media sites such as Linkedin, Twitter, and Facebook. Law firms are seeking their companies attention with tweets, videos, blog posts, pictures, and online content. Social media is fast and delivers news at record pace. This book provides you with a practical, goal-centric approach to using social media in your law practice that will enable you to identify social media platforms and tools that fit your practice and implement them easily, efficiently, and ethically.

iPad Apps in One Hour for Lawyers

By Tom Mighell

Product Code: 5110739 • **LPM Price:** $19.95 • **Regular Price:** $34.95

At last count, there were more than 80,000 apps available for the iPad. Finding the best apps often can be an overwhelming, confusing, and frustrating process. iPad Apps in One Hour for Lawyers provides the "best of the best" apps that are essential for any law practice. In just one hour, you will learn about the apps most worthy of your time and attention. This book will describe how to buy, install, and update iPad apps, and help you:

- Find apps to get organized and improve your productivity
- Create, manage, and store documents on your iPad
- Choose the best apps for your law office, including litigation and billing apps
- Find the best news, reading, and reference apps
- Take your iPad on the road with apps for travelers
- Maximize your social networking power
- Have some fun with game and entertainment apps during your relaxation time

Twitter in One Hour for Lawyers

By Jared Correia

Product Code: 5110746 • **LPM Price:** $24.95 • **Regular Price:** $39.95

More lawyers than ever before are using Twitter to network with colleagues, attract clients, market their law firms, and even read the news. But to the uninitiated, Twitter's short messages, or tweets, can seem like they are written in a foreign language. Twitter in One Hour for Lawyers will demystify one of the most important social-media platforms of our time and teach you to tweet like an expert. In just one hour, you will learn to:

- Create a Twitter account and set up your profile
- Read tweets and understand Twitter jargon
- Write tweets—and send them at the appropriate time
- Gain an audience—follow and be followed
- Engage with other Twitters users
- Integrate Twitter into your firm's marketing plan
- Cross-post your tweets with other social media platforms like Facebook and LinkedIn
- Understand the relevant ethics, privacy, and security concerns
- Get the greatest possible return on your Twitter investment
- And much more!

The Lawyer's Essential Guide to Writing

By Marie Buckley

Product Code: 5110726 • **LPM Price:** $47.95 • **Regular Price:** $79.95

This is a readable, concrete guide to contemporary legal writing. Based on Marie Buckley's years of experience coaching lawyers, this book provides a systematic approach to all forms of written communication, from memoranda and briefs to e-mail and blogs. The book sets forth three principles for powerful writing and shows how to apply those principles to develop a clean and confident style.

iPad in One Hour for Lawyers, Second Edition

By Tom Mighell

Product Code: 5110747 • **LPM Price:** $24.95 • **Regular Price:** $39.95

Whether you are a new or a more advanced iPad user, *iPad in One Hour for Lawyers* takes a great deal of the mystery and confusion out of using your iPad. Ideal for lawyers who want to get up to speed swiftly, this book presents the essentials so you don't get bogged down in technical jargon and extraneous features and apps. In just six, short lessons, you'll learn how to:

- Quickly Navigate and Use the iPad User Interface
- Set Up Mail, Calendar, and Contacts
- Create and Use Folders to Multitask and Manage Apps
- Add Files to Your iPad, and Sync Them
- View and Manage Pleadings, Case Law, Contracts, and other Legal Documents
- Use Your iPad to Take Notes and Create Documents
- Use Legal-Specific Apps at Trial or in Doing Research

30-DAY RISK-FREE ORDER FORM

LawPracticeManagementSection
MARKETING • MANAGEMENT • TECHNOLOGY • FINANCE

Please print or type. To ship UPS, we must have your street address. If you list a P.O. Box, we will ship by U.S. Mail.

Name

Member ID

Firm/Organization

Street Address

City/State/Zip

Area Code/Phone (In case we have a question about your order)

E-mail

Method of Payment:

☐ Check enclosed, payable to American Bar Association

☐ MasterCard ☐ Visa ☐ American Express

Card Number Expiration Date

Signature Required

MAIL THIS FORM TO:
American Bar Association, Publication Orders
P.O. Box 10892, Chicago, IL 60610

ORDER BY PHONE:
24 hours a day, 7 days a week:
Call 1-800-285-2221 to place a credit card order. We accept Visa, MasterCard, and American Express.

EMAIL ORDERS: orders@americanbar.org
FAX ORDERS: 1-312-988-5568

VISIT OUR WEB SITE: www.ShopABA.org
Allow 7-10 days for regular UPS delivery. Need it sooner? Ask about our overnight delivery options. Call the ABA Service Center at 1-800-285-2221 for more information.

GUARANTEE:
If–for any reason–you are not satisfied with your purchase, you may return it within 30 days of receipt for a refund of the price of the book(s). No questions asked.

Thank You For Your Order.

Join the ABA Law Practice Management Section today and receive a substantial discount on Section publications!

Product Code:	Description:	Quantity:	Price:	Total Price:
				$
				$
				$
				$
				$

**Shipping/Handling:	
$0.00 to $9.99	add $0.00
$10.00 to $49.99	add $5.95
$50.00 to $99.99	add $7.95
$100.00 to $199.99	add $9.95
$200.00 to $499.99	add $12.95

***Tax:**
IL residents add 9.75%
DC residents add 6%

Subtotal:	$
***Tax:**	$
****Shipping/Handling:**	$
Yes, I am an ABA member and would like to join the Law Practice Management Section today! (Add $50.00)	$
Total:	$